Seeds of Pr

Seeds of Promise

An Anthology of New Nature Writing

Editors:
Emma McKenzie
Julian Crooks

Illustrations by Sharon Williamson

All profits made from this book will be donated towards environmental charities.

Copyright © 2022 Emma McKenzie
All rights reserved.

ISBN: 9798844261589

All rights reserved to individual authors of the work included in this anthology. No part of this book may be reproduced or used in any manner without the prior written permission of the copyright owner, except for the use of brief quotations, which must be attributed to the individual author.

To request permissions contact **emma@lifeatbasecamp.com**

www.lifeatbasecamp.com

Edited by: Emma McKenzie and Julian Crooks

All illustrations, including the front cover, by Sharon Williamson © 2022

Photography by Tim Oxburgh © 2022

<u>Seeds of Promise</u>

<u>An Anthology of New Nature Writing</u>

With contributions from:

Rebecca Banks

Sarah Carlin

Jenny Cooper

Julian Crooks

Charlotte Dale

Phoebe Devenney

Elizabeth Fairweather

Nicky Hutchison

Sharon Linden

Katie Lloyd

Patricia Martin

Katherine Miskin

Steven Mitchell

Hilary Park

Kate Stacey

Suzanne Thomas

Berenice Tregenna

Sharon Williamson

Introductions by Emma McKenzie

Illustrations by Sharon Williamson

Seeds of Promise

An Anthology of New Nature Writing

Table of Contents

Introduction: 17

A Note from the Creative Writing Tutor: 19

DETAILS..21

Introduction: Details 23

Dandelion Clock by Rebecca Banks 25

Confetti by Charlotte Dale 25

Stump by Steven Mitchell 25

Beads of Autumn by Hilary Park 26

Tadpole by Julian Crooks 26

Overnight Snowfall by Sharon Williamson 26

Ivy Umbels Burst by Berenice Tregenna 27

What am I? by Sharon Linden 27

What am I? by Rebecca Banks 28

What am I? by Julian Crooks...28

A Refreshing Residence by Charlotte Dale 30

SPECIES 31

Introduction: Species *31*

Singing in the Rain by Steven Mitchell *35*

A Morning Song by Sharon Williamson *36*

A Hare's Perspective by Julian Crooks *37*

A Buzzard at Dawn by Sharon Linden *39*

Reynard's Sanctuary by Sarah Carlin *40*

A Room with a View by Sharon Linden *41*

The Night Watch by Sharon Williamson *42*

The Robin by Sharon Linden *43*

Blackbird by Nicky Hutchison *44*

Rockin' Robin by Nicky Hutchison *46*

Blackbird song by Charlotte Dale *47*

Centre Stage by Charlotte Dale *48*

Spider's Lacy Lair by Berenice Tregenna *49*

Spider's Web by Rebecca Banks *50*

Robin by Rebecca Banks *51*

Fire from Heaven by Hilary Park *52*

Cumbrian Beavers by Hilary Park *53*

Butterfly by Julian Crooks 54

Oracle of Hope by Julian Crooks 55

The Whitethroat by Julian Crooks 56

Unloved by Sarah Carlin 58

The Fox by Nicky Hutchison 60

Peregrine Paradise by Julian Crooks 62

My Friend by Steven Mitchell 63

Aerial (Larus argentatus) by Sarah Carlin 64

A Blackbird's Day by Elizabeth Fairweather 65

PLANTS AND TREES 67

Introduction: Plants and Trees 69

Driveway Dandelion by Rebecca Banks 70

A Nettle Leaf by Berenice Tregenna 71

The Ash Tree by Elizabeth Fairweather 72

Apple of my Eye by Nicky Hutchison 74

Letter to 'Our Oak Tree' by Charlotte Dale 76

Queen of My Garden by Rebecca Banks 77

The Mighty Ash by Julian Crooks 78

An Oak by Steven Mitchell 80

The Generous Rowan by Sharon Williamson..................................82

The Willow Tree by Sharon Linden..................................83

A Year in the Life of a Crab Apple by Jenny Cooper 85

GETTING HANDS ON IN NATURE 87

Introduction: Getting hands on in Nature 89

A Walk Round an Urban Garden by Elizabeth Fairweather 91

Summer Loving by Nicky Hutchison 93

Yet by Nicky Hutchison 94

Picnic at the Lighthouse by Steven Mitchell 95

On the Beach by Sharon Williamson 96

A Stormy Day by Sharon Williamson 97

Coastal Orchestra by Berenice Tregenna 98

I Forgot my Swimming Costume by Nicky Hutchison 99

Lost Connections by Rebecca Banks 102

Holding My Breath by Julian Crooks 103

The Lane by Julian Crooks 105

Forest Bathing by Julian Crooks 108

Hixbury Lane by Steven Mitchell 110

River Walk by Sharon Williamson 112

Inspirations from the Sea by Sharon Linden *113*

A Visit to Overhall Grove by Sharon Williamson *114*

Hedgerow Bathing by Suzanne Thomas *115*

Into the Forest by Katie Lloyd *116*

GETTING HANDS ON IN NATURE-HUMAN CONNECTION **117**

Sandcastles by Elizabeth Fairweather *119*

Dens by Steven Mitchell *120*

Feeding the Ducks by Nicky Hutchison *121*

Memory Trees by Hilary Park *122*

The Laburnum by Sharon Linden *123*

A Natural Christmas Present by Elizabeth Fairweather *124*

A Morning Dog Walk by Nicky Hutchison *125*

Pine Cone by Steven Mitchell *127*

The Official Water Collector by Rebecca Banks *128*

My Granny's Pond by Rebecca Banks *130*

Freewheeling on Cannock Chase by Rebecca Banks *131*

Childhood Landscape by Charlotte Dale *133*

In the Churchyard by Rebecca Banks *134*

A Haven Revisited by Sharon Linden *135*

July 1972 by Julian Crooks 137

That Robin's Back Again by Julian Crooks 139

A World of my Own by Sharon Linden......................................141

From Here to There – North Pennines by Hilary Park 143

Seaview by Sarah Carlin 144

FICTION WRITING 145

Introduction: Fiction Writing 147

The Lock by Patricia Martin 149

Misty Lake by Kate Stacey 150

The Lily Ponds and the Bumblebee by Patricia Martin 153

The Walled Garden by Sharon Williamson.................................155

Garden Date (a very short story) by Charlotte Dale....................156

Writing Inspired by the Film 'Kes' by Julian Crooks 157

A Lost World by Kate Stacey 158

Welcome to the Garden by Katherine Miskin............................163

Painting Masqueville Gardens by Katie Lloyd 167

The Tour of Tregurnock by Julian Crooks..................................169

What Happened Next at Tregurnock by Julian Crooks...............173

The Gardener's Secret by Julian Crooks......................................175

An introduction to: Landscape Writing Inspired by Photography 179

Landscape Photography by Tim Oxburgh....................................180

The Waterfall by Sharon Linden..182

A Fine Mist by Steven Mitchell..183

Waterfall by Hilary Park 184

Glinting by Sarah Carlin...186

Grey Boulders and Waterfalls by Rebecca Banks 187

The God of Anger by Nicky Hutchison 188

Wild by Katie Lloyd..189

The Green Valley by Sharon Williamson 190

Looking out at the View by Charlotte Dale.................................191

Manmade by Katie Lloyd...192

The Valley Floor by Patricia Martin...193

Landscape by Elizabeth Fairweather...195

Standing above the Treeline by Jenny Cooper............................197

The Shadows are Coming! by Berenice Tregenna.......................198

These Lumps of Stone by Julian Crooks 199

Tamed by Katie Lloyd 201

Introduction: Creating Images through Art 203

Almond Blossom by Katie Lloyd 204

The Walker by Sharon Williamson 205

Summer Fields by Katherine Miskin 206

Herdsman with Five Cows by a River 1650 to 1655 -   by Charlotte Dale 207

Saint-Rémy-de-Provence, July 1889 by Hilary Park 208

The Colour of My World by Julian Crooks 209

Bittersweet Vincent and Paul by Sarah Carlin 211

FOLKLORE, MYTHOLOGY AND FANTASY WRITING 215

Introduction: Folklore, Mythology and Fantasy Writing 217

Owls by Julian Crooks 219

White Heather by Phoebe Devenney 220

The Fen Tiger by Sharon Williamson 222

Myths and Folklore by Charlotte Dale 223

An Elemental Bird by Sharon Williamson 224

Foxgloves by Charlotte Dale 225

Breakfast with a Snaw-Grimet by Phoebe Devenney 226

Waking from Under the Hawthorn by Charlotte Dale 229

Elinor and the Hawthorn by Julian Crooks...................................*231*

All You Desire by Katherine Miskin *233*

The Lonely Black Bird by Nicky Hutchison *235*

Hagstone Haggle by Katie Lloyd *238*

The Legend of Wyre Forest and River Severn by Katie Lloyd.......*242*

The Uffington White Horse, Oxfordshire by Patricia Martin.......*244*

Under the Hawthorn Tree by Phoebe Devenney.........................*246*

Searching for Finn by Charlotte Dale...*250*

Benandonner's Revenge by Julian Crooks *251*

The Revenge of the Giant by Phoebe Devenney *255*

SCIENCE FICTION WRITING *257*

Introduction: Science Fiction Writing *259*

Kindred Spirit by Sharon Williamson..*261*

No Place Like Home by Charlotte Dale *262*

How Not to Conquer a Planet by Julian Crooks *264*

About the Editors: *267*

About the Writers:..*268*

Getting Started on Nature Writing *274*

Useful Links and Resources..*276*

15

Introduction:

This anthology comprises a selection of writings produced in response to tasks from two creative writing courses offered by the Field Studies Council in the late Spring and Summer of 2021. The course titles: 'Exploring Nature Writing' and 'Developing Nature Writing' indicate the focus. Each course ran consecutively for 4 weeks with a short break between them. For me, and I'm sure other students, these courses came at just the right time. The recent pandemic and the lockdowns that ensued resulted in millions of us seeking out interactions with nature either as a welcome solace or much needed distraction from such troubling times.

A key component of the nature writing courses was to submit our pieces, written in response to 3 or 4 creative writing tasks each week, to an online forum for all participants to read and comment upon. This would be followed up at the end of each week by an online zoom meeting hosted by Emma McKenzie during which pieces were discussed by all. It was clear that tutor and students alike were bound together by our shared love of nature and the joy of creative writing. I found myself uplifted and exhilarated – by both the variety of tasks and topics and the different approaches taken by students and the sheer quality of much of the writing. These weekly zoom sessions represented an oasis of empathy and positivity that seemed to simply ooze from my computer screen.

I hope that the pieces selected here provide as much pleasure to you the reader as they did for us the writers.

Julian Crooks

A Note from the Creative Writing Tutor:

Emma McKenzie

Connecting to nature through close observation using writing and drawing was an idea first discussed by Ruskin (1819–1900) who, way ahead of his time, taught us that to observe nature was to open a door to curiosity, to understand better our roots and connection with nature. Through teaching drawing Ruskin taught his students to appreciate the fine details of their surroundings, to look at the world with curiosity and to build on their appreciation of the world.[1]

As a writer and artist interested in nature, I approach the written word very much as I would approach creating a painting. First, I gather my 'sketches' of the natural world with words, before building up to working those sketches into larger bodies of work that draw on the finer details to produce an accurate image and feeling of the natural world around us.

Not only has this helped me to develop a rich understanding of the natural world, but it has also helped to spark my curiosity and continue my journey to write well and to make new discoveries and understandings in my writing practice.

---

[1] As discussed in To See Clearly: Why Ruskin Matters, by Suzanne Fagence Cooper, Published by Quercus Books Feb 2019.

The following anthology is therefore set out in a similar way. We begin with the small details, taking you through small sketches with words, before looking in focus at trees, plant species and animals. We then move on to include work that begins with personal interactions getting hands on in nature, before moving on to fiction writing. The final two chapters draw on folklore, mythology and fantasy writing, and science fiction.

I hope that you will find this body of work both inspiring and interesting. I have set out a short introduction to each section to set the scene and context of how the work was produced. Finally at the end of the book there are a few writing tasks to help get you started with your own words.

DETAILS

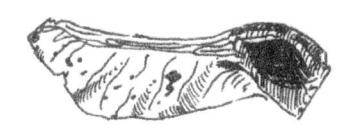

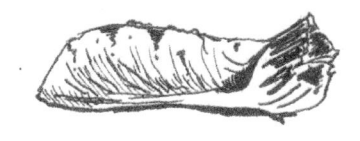

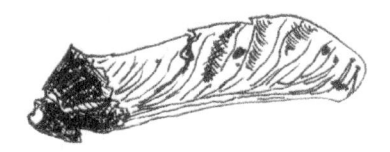

Introduction: Details

How many times have you walked past a snail and noticed whether the spiral of its shell turns to the right or left? If you take a moment to stop and look, you will discover that the majority twist to the right (righties) and only a few to the left (lefties), as with our own left- or right-handed dominance. If you stopped to look at that, you might then observe that some shells are brown and speckle striped, like the markings of a tabby cat. Others are cream and delicate brown stripes, some orange. Once you start noticing snails, for more than just a garden pest, you will begin to discover where they like to rest and that their silvery trails often criss-cross many times over the same path, sometimes looping around the same curve. But have you tried to find one in winter? Good luck if you do try, for they are nowhere to be found, hidden, tucked deep away, sheltering in deep crevices and cracks. I once found over a hundred wedged deeply inside a dead tree stump.

Before you realise it, you will have opened an endless micro-world of curiosity and questions that only lead to more discoveries. If you take notice of the small details and take time to observe, you will never have a bored moment. In a story, a tiny detail can speak volumes to a reader about the setting, the character and the situation. A small detail in the right place can offer an insight, spark curiosity, ignite the imagination and vividly bring an image to life.

Details can also be a brilliant place to begin a story. Imagine one tiny blown seed head from a dandelion, smaller than a grain of rice with its own feathered parachute. How far can that seed travel? Where might it land and grow? What does the journey look like? A story thread begins to unravel before your eyes.

This section starts with the tiniest form of poetry, a haiku. Haiku originated in Japan and are made up of 17 syllables, usually working to three lines of 5,7,5 syllables. Traditional haiku often capture seasonal changes and details. For more information see our useful links at the end of the book.

Dandelion Clock by Rebecca Banks

(A haiku)

Seeds of promise cling,

Jostling in the gentle breeze.

Gone! Blown to mark time.

Confetti by Charlotte Dale

(A haiku)

Blossom confetti
Showers of spring, then wind blows,
Fall – confetti leaves.

Stump by Steven Mitchell

(A haiku)

Stump, rotten and damp

Flaking, dissolving away

While fungi feast well.

Beads of Autumn by Hilary Park

(A haiku)

Through deep tangled copse

Bright beads of Autumn glisten

Simple scarlet hope

Tadpole by Julian Crooks

(A haiku)

Waving frantic tail

Hungry tadpole changing, then

Three months: frog on stone

Overnight Snowfall by Sharon Williamson

(A haiku)

Overnight snowfall

Betrays countless wanderings –

And then melts away

Ivy Umbels Burst by Berenice Tregenna

(A haiku)

Ivy umbels burst

Buzzing bees and butterflies

Silence – nectar gone...

What am I? by Sharon Linden

Silent, scentless, long and rounded. Feather-light with coppery hue. Covered with soft, pointed, paper-thin scales catching on my skin. The slightest movement and its children are scattered everywhere.[2]

---

[2] Answer: Spruce Cone

What am I? by Rebecca Banks

It sits there quietly on the wayside, half-hidden amidst the wilting daffodils. A discarded, broken, pure white cup, full of nothing now, except hope and questions. A white cup, with a jagged rim, more fragile and beautiful than the most delicate ceramic, it lies there forgotten, like the detritus of an argument, or celebration. It is light, almost weightless, yet its unexpected strength affords new beginnings. [3]

What am I? by Julian Crooks

It resembles the blade of a spear and is 14 centimetres long from the base of the stem to the pointed tip. From the end of the stem the blade broadens gradually to 2.5 centimetres at its widest point before narrowing to the tip. Five veins extend along the length of the blade. The third of these, in the middle of the blade, runs along the centre as straight as a die; the others outside of it on either side curve gently away from the centre before coming inwards to meet at the tip. On the underside of the blade the five veins stand proud from the surface resembling the steel ribs on the keel of an ocean

---

[3] Answer: A broken egg shell.

liner; consequently, as you turn it over, the veins on the top surface give the appearance of being recessed. The surface is smooth otherwise, but the tips of your gentle fingers allow you to feel the slightest, slightest sensation of miniscule hairs carpeting it. Very close inspection reveals a number of round pin pricks randomly scattered, each one completely piercing the blade.[4]

---

[4] Answer: Ribwort Plantain

A Refreshing Residence by Charlotte Dale

Must be viewed – this dwelling is well presented, compact (if a frog) and spacious (if a water flea). This suburban garden sanctuary lets in plenty of light in the upper storey with dark cover below. Well presented, with fragrant watermint, marsh marigold and pebbles for plenty of shelter and easy access. This quiet, homely, fully furnished water body can be used as a permanent residence or seasonal getaway. **NB** – please note it is occasionally used by avian visitors for bathing and passing thirsty mammals.

SPECIES

Introduction: Species

When Robert MacFarlane and Jackie Morris[5] created *The Lost Words* poetry book for children, they were aiming to raise awareness of fifty words naming things from the natural world that were due to be removed from the Oxford Children's Dictionary. If we don't have language to describe something, that thing becomes lost and unknown. When we use words to name and describe things, those things become present in our everyday interactions and our daily lives. To raise awareness of the insects, animals and species that live alongside us we considered the natural world from different perspectives. Choosing tasks that encouraged the writers to consider the micro world of insects, through to re-imagining a daily walk from the perspective of the species in our local area opened up new understandings and awareness of those species living beside us. We also considered those species who have a bad reputation and re-considered the stories that we tell about them. Did you know for example that wasps are important pollinators and that snails generally do more damage to the garden than a slug? Narratives and stories are powerful. Using writing we can reconsider our place in the world alongside those with which we share it.

---

[5] The Lost Words, by Robert MacFarlane and Jackie Morris. Published by Hamish Hamilton Publishers, 2017.

You will notice that this section has a number of poems about robins; this was because one of the tasks focused on creating poetry featured a robin as our subject. Just like in our gardens, we thought it would be fun to pepper the section with robins, as each writer created their own distinct take on this beautiful bird.

Singing in the Rain by Steven Mitchell

It must see me

Hooded from the rain

Vapour cloud breath

Camera lens extended.

Yet, it perches

Matchstick legs

On bare branches

Ink eyed, and face flushed

Its tawny wings twitching

Singing like no-one's watching.

A Morning Song by Sharon Williamson

On a grey winter morning

Amid the buzz of traffic and passing people

A robin sits high in the bare branches

And casts his clear notes into the day.

Watching, listening, ever alert,

Feathers fluffed against the cool, damp air

He sings variations on a theme,

Sweet phrases that say: 'I am here!'

Does anyone hear him? Is anyone moved?

One small songbird lost in the humdrum of humanity,

The robin pauses

Then sings on, regardless.

A Hare's Perspective by Julian Crooks

I'm the Lord of this field. I can see everything from here. This is a large arable field, newly seeded, maybe five acres or so and my mate and I are right in the middle. She's got her head down now in the newly seeded crop, picking out seeds and fresh sprung shoots, so I'm up on my haunches keeping lookout. I only need to turn my head now and again; you see my eyes are positioned right on the side and towards the top of my head so my field of vision (pardon the pun) is nearly 360°. Plus I have such lovely long ears – they're not just for show, you know – they can pick up really tiny sounds, footsteps in the distance, a fox slyly negotiating its way through brambles, so we're alerted to dangers early.

You might think it odd that we don't scuttle down a burrow like our cousins the rabbits, but we don't need burrows and warrens. These huge hind legs have such powerful muscles we can sprint like the wind and if we do have to lie still then we can become invisible! Our camouflage is so convincing we can settle down into these hollowed out depressions called forms and when we lie still chances are you'd step on us before you saw us.

So even though we are right in the middle of this field we feel pretty safe. I automatically check out escape routes if we do sense a threat: towards and into the thickly wooded copse on one side, the hedgerows on two other sides and down the slope to that tree-lined stream on the fourth side. I think I'll stay Lord of this field a little while yet.

A Buzzard at Dawn by Sharon Linden

As the sun slowly rises on a damp and chilly morning, atop a crumbling old fencepost I sit. It has been a cold night and so I perch, wings outspread, basking in its warmth.

With the stiffness of the morning now seeping away, I take to the skies in search of food. With my wings spread wide, wingtips upturned, I gently soar over the world below.

Beneath me, winding away to the left like a thin strand of cotton, a dry and dusty pathway, the line of demarcation between the world of humans, and ours. I scout the land, eyes peeled, looking for the smallest of movements in fields and hedgerows. Everything looks so small and insignificant from up here, and peaceful too as the air currents bear me along.

Something flickers in the field below, so I circle down to investigate... the sun, reflecting off something discarded by man. But wait, I see something familiar, over there behind those rocks. Alighting on the topmost stone, I see my favourite meal. Not a live creature, as most would believe, but the abandoned remains of a tired old rabbit, who has lived his life to the full... and so, I dine.

Reynard's Sanctuary by Sarah Carlin

All was still and calm in the old railway garden. The train tracks that had once felt loud huffing engines, were now overgrown with grass and wildflowers. The bees were softly buzzing about their essential work.

Standing alert on my four paws, I sniffed the air. A rabbit may be downwind, but too far away to bother chasing in the heat of this summer's day.

I trot over to where the old station's platform was. There is an intriguing metal pot that I've not noticed before, a spout at one end. I stick my head in and find a cool pool of water inside. Dropping my tongue, I lap up a refreshing scoop, licking my lips.

The pungent smell of lavender greets me and I decided to have a snooze in my favourite spot under the shade of this bush. I settled down in a curl of my ginger fur and admire the little garden before me, just before my eyes start to droop.

Centaurea cyanus, papaver, Leucanthemum vulgare, Ranunculus.

This really is my favourite place. It has a little shed with a conveniently sized hole that I sometimes take refuge in if it's raining, a patch of grass that I enjoy rolling on to play, and a heap of soft earth that I can dig in. There's also a little orchard at one end, and the fallen apples in the autumn make for a tasty treat.

When the humans are not around, it is a fox's sanctuary!

A Room with a View by Sharon Linden

I am sure he doesn't mean to boast, but ever since Squirrel moved into his new abode, he has definitely been strutting around with his thick, bushy tail a little higher than those of the others, and a very definite twinkle in his eye.

If you shade your eyes and follow the twisting trunk of the old oak, there, safely anchored in the fork of three strong branches, you will find his pride and joy.

Old twigs intertwined, earthy smelling moss and old leaves pushed deep into any gaps to keep the drafts at bay. Inside, a thick underlay of damp leaves? Nature's underfloor heating! (All the mod cons for Squirrel!), and of course, last of all, the deepest of carpets. Layers of rich, autumnal leaves giving a warm cosy glow within these snug and rustic walls.

Maybe, just maybe though, his pride and joy are not this penthouse delight, with breath-taking vista without. If you focus your eyes deep into the hollow within, you may just catch the slightest glimpse of three little ones, snuggled down, sleeping soundly, safe from the dangers below.

The Night Watch by Sharon Williamson

As the sun goes down so my day begins, with a wing stretch and a hop out of my roost. All is in good order, so I glide away in silence to the familiar perches and hunting grounds: the grassy meadow, the verges and the paddock, the peaceful fringes of the village and the farm. I float along the field edges, then drop like a stone onto a rustling in the grass – ever hungry, ever driven to find my next meal. When prey is plentiful I'll prosper; when the hunting is poor, then I'll fly the line of starvation, always listening for the next shiver in the grass.

The Robin by Sharon Linden

Small and round the fellow sits

On branches stripped bare by Autumn's hands.

His dull, brown suit is stretched to its limit, a dashing crimson cravat,

Bursting from a straining pale grey waistcoat,

Reflecting a fiery blush across his face.

"Does anyone speak my tongue?" he flutes,

With a flick of his head as his eyes scan the woods.

Reverberating back on a chilly breeze, "Hello, I understand!"

And there he passes the time of day,

As the waters below carry his song away.

Blackbird by Nicky Hutchison

It's a porthole framed by twigs and sweet leaves in a dark, calm Lonicera hedge. Confined in my sculpted cup, I brood and watch the sea of life wash by. Birds land, chirp and flit on the haggard stone wall across the path. Rabbits in the field beyond hop, then skitter if danger approaches. There is a lot of 'cry wolf' but you never know. One dark morning, a great beast snuffled at my window. The two commas of his wet nose tried to inhale me and then a white giant stared in with its saucer eyes and a bright light. I did not move and I do not think they saw me but it feels unsafe. The eternal progress of the night and day is like the slowest blink of an eye shot through with flashes of colour that pass my viewpoint. The rush of an engine or snatches of chat rise and fall in the come and go. You never get the full story here, just a glimpse of the now.

A whisper of smoke, a scent of cherry blossom, the earthy hit of a deer or badger on the breeze, briefly tangs the dark green air in the hedge, then leaches away.

    The grumble of metal from the big road is a humming backdrop until the deep night curtain falls and you sense the land exhale. The trees exchange their news along the forest floor and only the snap of a twig, the scratch of a shrew or the breath catch of a quick fox betrays the busy night shift.

The criss-cross network of the bush protects me from the outside world but I know all the escape routes and tonight it is my time to go.

Rockin' Robin by Nicky Hutchison

There's a dash of glamour in the dull, damp dawn

A bright, quick life in the still forlorn

Fierce hematite beadies and tomato soup bib

With tight clutch talons and stiletto nib

Robin dips and darts to catch the news

Then cheeps away his short sharp views.

A town crier above white traffic noise

Reminding us of simpler joys

Robin's there, king of his 'hood

Cock of the walk, the park and wood.

Blackbird song by Charlotte Dale

I have the best spot. The dawn breeze has a chill and it blows my fine black feathers around the top of my legs. I fill my lungs of cool clear air from this high conifer tree. Below is the robin, he sings too from the street lamp. I make sure my song carries across rooftops, through branches in the trees and louder than my neighbours. I grip onto the branch and sing – getting louder as below me the drone of machines moves along grey pathways. The air is no longer clear and each breath tastes of acrid metal. But I stay and sing – this is my territory.

Centre Stage by Charlotte Dale

Needle-like beak,

open and close.

Sweet sounding notes

tumble and flow.

Orange red breast;

beacon of light,

he takes centre stage

all day and all night.

Spider's Lacy Lair by Berenice Tregenna

There she is, tucked away in her kingdom with the verdant backdrop of leaves and grass. This woven tapestry is self-made. The embroidered pattern looks very organised in its circular design. There is a quiet order to her surrounds and it is well-presented in uniformly spaced lines.

    She sits proudly in the centre, admiring her work and waits. In the shade, it is easy to miss and looks like a deceptively weak build. Although, those that are unfortunate enough to visit, will feel trapped and realise it is a sturdy structure after all. Once they have been lured into this lacy lair…

Spider's Web by Rebecca Banks

Delicately draped across the fringes of a hedgerow, the dwelling is a masterclass in DIY construction. This organised home is assembled with precision, almost algebraic in its intricacy. Best viewed in the ethereal quiet of the sunrise when the hoarfrost clings to each silvery, silky strand.

    Each web is individually crafted by an arachnid artisan, with strong natural fibres woven with care to create a fine sticky filigree. Excellent for when winged neighbours visit for dinner.

Robin by Rebecca Banks

My Granny's favourite,

For its cheek and cheer,

Amidst the depths of the darker months.

He perches, puffed up and proud on budded branches,

Chattering commandingly,

Trilling with tenacity,

Head tipping,

Toes gripping.

Catching the answers to his call.

My favourite now.

Amidst the depths of the darker months,

The robin ignites a flame of remembrance.

And brings a hint of hopefulness,

To us all.

Fire from Heaven by Hilary Park

You sing Robin and the painting lives;

turning to reveal your breast-burnt,

you perch on a brushstroke,

light as a church whisper

your ever bright eyes piercing,

each glance a black note on life's stave.

Sharp listening all the while

a flute on the air catches you fast,

you inhale and fill with nightingale's song.

A sweet bird our Robin, but mettlesome -

your feathers an ash smudge save threat red,

underneath round, grey-linted

soft ruffling white on a winter breeze.

Those fire-soaked myths of wren and thorn

follow you through the deep woods

but you stay, beloved close to home.

Cumbrian Beavers by Hilary Park

It took us two days to complete the lodge using local trees, stones and mud – that includes excavating the deep water filled corridors leading from the wood to our hall. The location we were brought to by Jim (our conservation manager) is a secluded woodland (apparently we have 27 acres), it's quiet with an excellent pond. However, the lodge he'd prepared for us was really more of a starter home for beavers and my husband Glen and I, we're past *that* stage. Jim isn't a beaver so how could he know that we need a roomy home with two underwater entrances and at least two grass-lined rooms, all vented of course. The dark damp is fine for us (we've moved from Scotland) and the easy access to mixed trees which we harvest is ideal. We've already coppiced lots of birch trees and stuck them firmly in the mud underwater near our back door, I call it our winter larder.

So we feel safe and happy here; this is our dream lodge really, rustic and homely and made completely from recycled material. Jim said he is thrilled with our dam building.

Butterfly by Julian Crooks

Goggle-eyed at its dayglo-green undulations, the caterpillar

was tenderly plucked and lovingly rehomed in an old shoebox

(thoughtfully furnished with dandelions and docks)

Next morning a grubby parchment package had taken its place.

My mother spun me a silken story of a Cinderella beauty emerging

from the ugly, coarse and shrunken husk.

How could this wizened pod give birth to such a bloom?

Now, my eight year-old self and I gawp

At wire-spun legs and blushing, courtesan fans.

Oracle of Hope by Julian Crooks

Oil-spot eyes, bib of winter fire, he holds our

gaze: 'Listen to this ...' and out

bubbles the sweetest tones, tinkling, rilling,

                        tripping and dipping

                                    cas

                                  ca

                                      ding

                                            and stop!!

No, a pause – (as though he has quite forgotten the words, or the tune, or both)
And then the sweetest repeat: persistent, plaintiff, pleading.
Yes, he laments the summer past on this bare, January twig but under
his tight-clawed grasp, surging magically up through those slant-black legs he
senses the rise of hawthorn sap. A melancholy song.
Oracle of Hope.

The Whitethroat by Julian Crooks

A (very) long time ago I remember my father giving me one of his occasional pearls of wisdom: 'If you've got something to say, just say it.' This, I have since discovered, is generally good advice. Age and experience has taught me that in many situations there is nothing to be gained from hesitancy; you just have to grasp the nettle and say it!

The whitethroat doesn't suffer from such socially conditioned repression. He says just what he wants to say. In fact he belts it out! His song is rather short and staccato, scratchy and rushed. But that's only due to the fact that his message is really quite simple: to male whitethroats – 'Keep out this is my territory!' and to female whitethroats – 'Here I am ladies!' He is the perfect role model for us all – just say what you want to say and make sure they hear you.

Like the town crier of yore he picks his best vantage point from which to proclaim, normally (unlike said crier) atop a bush. His plumage is eye-catching. A fabulous combination of pale underneath, a darker grey mantle above, rufous wing coverts, the cutest of white throats contrasting with the subtle slate blue-grey head. When sharing his message he often goes the extra mile and raises his crest. This little guy definitely wants to be seen and heard.

Yes, there are lots of warblers which define our spring and delight us with their wonderful and varied songs: eloquent and elongated, convoluted and subtle, though sadly many hide away and can be frustratingly difficult to see – nightingales and garden warblers being good examples. Mr Whitethroat, on the other hand, is devoid of inhibitions, he doesn't know the meaning of the word 'skulk'; he wants to be seen and heard! There are not many more thrilling experiences on a spring morning than to hear his staccato scratch in the distance and, as you approach, to be rewarded by this splendid vision of confident, assertive self-assuredness. Loud and proud, he says just what he wants to say! So don't be shy – just say it.[6]

---

[6] Here's a link to a video for you to enjoy the sight and sound of Mr Whitethroat: https://www.youtube.com/watch?v=-Rerxw9vloo

Unloved by Sarah Carlin

Hello, do you think you know me?

You don't care for me, yet you love those bees.

You call me by some ugly names...

Vespula vulgaris, vespa crabro - polistes satan!

People swat us, drown us,

Imprison us under glass.

Bemoan that we gatecrash your picnics,

It's our sugar cravings that fuel us to be fast.

Buzzing, bothersome and brash

You don't like to see my yellow and black striped jacket,

Come near your trash.

But I am not pointless, I am precious.

We've hung out with the dinosaurs,

Well before you humans graced this earth.

We don't all sting, and some of us only when we are provoked.

Some of us are just so tiny, known as fairyflies - mymaridae.

We have an important job to do and

We feed on those aphids that annoy your lovely flowers.

I could save your life - my saliva has antibiotic properties and

One day, I may even have a cure for cancer.

But am I disappearing fast?
It feels like no-one has bothered to ask.
My climate is changing, my home being destroyed,
And the pesticides you use are choking me inside.

Do you know what you are doing?
Because I really do play a vital ecological role,
I am a valuable pollinator.
Please don't waste us wasps, let us labour on.

The Fox by Nicky Hutchison

Early one morning, the fox stood on a hillock overlooking the mountain lake. A sugar-coating of snow frosted the grass. The air was paused and frozen. The gun metal lake rippled slightly, rearranging its secrets, and the stark trees stood petrified in gangs or clung to the water's edge, as if that would save them, now the time had come. Higher up, the hills were laid bare. No trees could bear the howling gales that beset the tops. No living thing would withstand the keening of wraiths that flew across each night.

The fox's nose twitched, hoping for a snatch of rabbit scent or easy meal of a stray dead sheep that had not made it off the merciless hill. He padded on the springy mix of turf and moss and looked to the blank sky for clues. His eyes followed a raven kiting high in the white sky. If there was carrion to be had, the bird would be lower. He would have to do his own hunting this morning before the rush of runners and walkers laboured up to the top, oblivious of mountain magic and the swimmers who would recklessly slip through cracks in the tarn's mirror unaware that they were courting catastrophe. He pawed at half a scrappy crow's wing that lay on the pebble path but no flesh remained. As the ice crept into his bones, the fox picked up pace heading for the stone walls higher up that would protect him from the worst. He was the only vibrant spot of colour in the landscape. The land here had had its blood slowly leached away until the yellow and browns lay depleted of vibrancy and life. Her.

The fragile skin of silence was suddenly torn by the screeching of a sparrowhawk as it dive-bombed behind the horizon. Suddenly, from behind the hill, dozens of urgent ravens surged into the air, the panic palpable even from where the fox crouched at the crossroads of lichen-scarred stone walls. She was here. The fox slunk back down to the tree line and circled the lake. On the brow, on an old mossed coffin stone, he saw it. Two rows of super-sized smooth stone teeth, arranged in a permanent rictus. She had defeated the giant and all that was left of him was a mouthful of molars, grey with age but whitened on the crowns from feasting on the bones of the dead. They were for it now.

Peregrine Paradise by Julian Crooks

One of the top locations in this sought after urban hotspot the peregrine nest box offers a multitude of benefits to the peregrine couple looking to raise a growing family. With its stylish, largely open format construction of well-weathered purpose built pine planking, this must see penthouse apartment offers unrivalled views over the city below and all around. In the far distance the owners can make out the moors and hills of the Peak District – a reminder of a traditionally 'natural' setting, but this observation tower attached to the side and close to the top of St George's church tower has a scenic setting second to none. The city's larder of pigeons is just a short stoop away, so providing for those ever hungry youngsters is never going to be a problem. Yes, the nestbox might be dirty, the grit-covered floor infested with fleas and insects feeding on faeces and bits of left over pigeons and the like, but its airy, well ventilated aspect eradicates foul odours. So see for yourself how a shelf with sides can become a peregrine's own platform paradise![7]

---

[7] To book a viewing follow the link: http://peregrine.group.shef.ac.uk/

My Friend by Steven Mitchell

On a wintery morning—a hat, scarf, gloves, thick coat, woolly socks morning—icy wind slapping my face, and the weak sun suffocating behind clouds, I discover brightness. Perched on a bare hedgerow branch, a robin, its orange-red breast a beacon of colour in the dullness, twitters its bright song. I stop and greet it. And it returns my hello, nodding its little head and bouncing towards me on skinny legs. I try to entice it to rest on my outstretched hand, but I'm happy it's close enough to tell me I'm its friend, before it flits away to find others to cheer. And for the rest of the day, I try to be a little more robin.

Aerial (*Larus argentatus*) by Sarah Carlin

As I launch upwards and feel the cool breeze licking my underwings, I look down. The sea looks different from my lofty hover – it is a moving mass, immense and ethereal.

It smells different too up here compared to back onshore, the tingly saltiness is more pungent, filling my olfactory glands. No pong of fish and chips here, only the sweet scent of seaweed and cleaner air.

I soar, an airy spirit, free, and yet in danger.

The sound of the waves echo and fall, but they appear more muffled from on high. I see the bob of flotsam and jetsam, and the plastic undulating down below.

What lies beneath? Hidden in these watery graves down in the deep. I spy movement and let out a raucous shriek!

Swirling down like a dervish, I crash clumsily onto the surface, and gobble a tasty echinoderm in my beak.

A Blackbird's Day by Elizabeth Fairweather

My day starts really early, just before dawn. I sing from the top of the aerial to warn all the other blackbirds around this is my space.

I have to tell you it's a tricky life being a blackbird. You have to keep all your wits about you all the time. So many hazards. And you often wonder if you can find enough to eat. It's especially difficult at this time of year – breeding season.

My partner and I have three little ones. They are almost as big as we grown-ups now, able to fly a little bit to get themselves out of trouble. But can they feed themselves? I'm constantly on the hunt for another tasty titbit to plunge into one yellow gape or another.

And they're constantly one hop behind me... or even one in front of me, chirping out for more.

The only way to escape is to fly off. But then my partner would not half twitter on about it. And she's sitting on more eggs!

Ah! I know that human just over there. Maybe she's brought food for us?

I feel like I know every blade of grass in this garden, the number of times I've hopped over it.

Oh well, round up the youngsters, then a quick song from the aerial or the tree and then to bed.

PLANTS AND TREES

Introduction: Plants and Trees

Do you have a favourite tree? One you notice year in, year out? Do you know what type of species it is? How about plants and flowers? Is there a particular plant that reminds you of a family member, or a particular event in your life?

Each day we rush about our busy lives barely taking the time to notice the beautiful plants and trees that surround us. Many of us take for granted the rhythms and cycles of nature. The delicate opening of flowers on a bright morning, the changing colours of leaves as we step into autumn. Nature's miracles are happening constantly, all around us.

When I started to write about the natural world, I started to become curious, to know how long a tree had been growing for, to learn the names of my green neighbours that line the paths to my workplace. To understand how one tiny handful of dust-blown seeds can create a meadow of wildflowers, so rich in colour.

The tasks that created the following pieces of work were focused on taking time to notice the plants and trees around us. To consider the seasons and the rhythms of nature, to appreciate the resilience of the natural world and nature's ability to find room for itself and prosper in the most unlikely places.

Driveway Dandelion by Rebecca Banks

I have worked hard to be here. I have pushed and squeezed and wrenched and exploded into view, through a tiny fissure, a crack of concrete. A fraction of light caught my attention and I fought to bask in the warmth and nourishment. And now, here I am, a scrap of something beautifully organic, in a world of grey, throwing roots south to find life.

From where I grow, I can see the coarse solid stone through which I burst. I have a prickly neighbour to whom I nod cheerfully at from time to time. If I tilt my sunshine head upwards, I see an endless blue. Each day, I see the same sets of shoes scramble, plod, or streak past me. From my discrete place in the world, I hear snippets of conversations…

"Did you hear about old Mrs Watson, she's terribly ill…"

"Hurry up, Emily, we're going to be late…"

"We'll sort the front out next week, get some of these weeds up."

I have worked hard to be here… yet I fear my days are numbered.

Let's pray for rain.

A Nettle Leaf by Berenice Tregenna

The sun is beating down and I stretch out my veins to reach towards the light. I wonder if I'll have a visitor today? I watch and wait. Suddenly, there they are, crawling up the stem. A bright red button moving up and up, getting closer and closer. Until, there it is, the tell-tale tickling sensation. They have arrived. They take a bit of time to settle on me but they are home now. They seem happy to sit on my soft, green ridges with their little legs tucked under them. I am proud they chose me. I must be comfortable. Overhead, there is more activity, the buzzing around the petalled bells above makes me smile. Someone is getting their food today. I am sure it is harder work being a flower. Although, sometimes I can be the centre of activity, remembering when the little red button above me laid its eggs on my underside from which little creatures grew. That got a bit sticky! I thought they would never leave. I prefer it when they are older and sit still on me. Unless they are eating the very small green things that have been known to nibble...Ouch! That's when I am glad to have some movement. Today is restful though and I'm loving it as I watch the crawling in the earth beneath me...

The Ash Tree by Elizabeth Fairweather

I have been standing here for around 300 years. In the beginning, I was surrounded by fields full of crops and animals; part of a large farm, and I remember watching people scurrying about around me. A hedge spread out like arms either side of me. There were several other trees dotted about.

In the spring, the warmer air would rise up to greet me and envelope me. Gradually, I felt my bright, finger-like leaves gently open to adorn my branches with green. How grand it was to wave them about.

Then, as the leaves completely cloaked me, some little birds would come and build their nests among my branches. How proud I felt to be charged with their care.

Summer came and I found another use for my leafy branches – helping me to keep cool as the heat intensified.

In the autumn, my leaves would fall, leaving me adorned solely with my precious cargo of seeds, neatly packaged in a papery, brown casing.

Winters would come and go, snow softly falling on my leafless frame and edging my branches with white icing. Gradually, the seed packets would tumble to the ground and birds and small animals would carry some of them away. I hope some of the seeds managed to find a nurturing home deep within the earth.

But, in more recent years, the farmland has shrunk. A grey snake now runs behind me and when the metal boxes go roaring past along it, it makes my whole being quiver.

More and more, the crops and animals have gone and been replaced by buildings.

I shudder each time I see more huge, metal monsters come to dig more holes and deliver more materials. They are getting nearer.

Apple of my Eye by Nicky Hutchison

The three crones stand mute, as if frozen mid-conversation. Surely they will not have survived the cold this time? Their scraped, bent torsos are rough with pale iced green lichen, their arms arthritic-looking with twisted knots and knuckles. They look dead on their feet in the quiet, silent embrace of winter's chill.

As the bridal train of winter slides out of sight, the temperatures rise. The crones stretch their aching bones and erupt with tiny green shoots which cannot hide their tortured skeletons. Then, deep pink buds, the colour of old ladies' lipstick appear and open to a wedding celebration of blush-stained white blossom. The crones are transformed anew into frivolous, fresh-faced girls laughing in the Spring breezes where goldfinches and sparrows sway.

In summer, impossibly, their round, dimpled, red-cheeked children appear holding tightly to their mothers' fingers. In the evening light, the apples glow and seem to enchant, like the portentous feature of a fairy tale waiting for a human to falter. Come autumn, the children have succumbed. Many lie rotting on the ground, pecked out by birds or nibbled by mice. Blossom and leaves are brown and sodden, downtrodden. Magic has fled and it is like a battlefield where the trees have lost. They retreat into themselves for the winter once again.

And there they stand, stark-naked and bereft. But this year, a new spell is cast. Yellow-green mistletoe seems to magically emerge from withered skin and hangs with a translucent pearl at the centre of each wishbone like an elaborate necklace. Under its dancing legs, I plant a kiss on my dog's head to ward off bad luck, and because it's Christmas.

Letter to 'Our Oak Tree' by Charlotte Dale

I try to recall when I first noticed you. Was it your wide ivy clad trunk, home and forage to an array of wildlife? Or was it your majestic crown I view from my bedroom window each morning? Above the rooftops and chimney pots your branches are outstretched – a calming peaceful view amongst the brickwork of a housing estate.

Each time I walk past you throughout the seasons I gaze at your beauty. In winter, your bare outstretched branches have little 'paws' on the end, ready to burst into bud in the coming months. Then once unfurled in spring, they give way to the unmistakable lobed leaves. Why is it with other plants and trees I feel a sadness at the end of summer, but with you it's different? Because in the autumn your beauty and bounty reward us all – human and animal. As shoes crunch on your fallen acorns against the tarmac, wildlife stock their winter larder – and I, like the other 364 days gaze at your beauty.

Queen of My Garden by Rebecca Banks

Adored by mammal, insect and bird alike, she is majestic in her stance, generous in her bounty. Look closely, at this time of year, the fine, delicate branch tips are adorned with tiny, pointed buds, a royal reddish tinge to these sun seeking shoots. She stands tall, watchful over a pair of pigeons performing zestful gymnastics on the border fence.

As the sun warms her hopeful buds, lime green leaves burst forth creating a domed canopy-crown worthy of any queen. Tasselled catkins hang gently, waiting for the breeze to carry them forth. Her shade provides sweet comfort for her human and four-legged subjects beneath her branches. As the leaves darken and their light hair is lost, the glory of the beech tree is at its peak.

Her late summer mast ripens now. A squirrel gathers greedily at her feet. Her gifts fall, making way for the bronzing of the leaves, a spectacle so beautiful, it sets the sky on fire. And these leaves fall, like treasure, leaving mountains of gold.

Her skin is smooth, grey, etched with lines of the passing years. And as icy wind descends, she stands empty and bereft, stoic and tough, before her strength is renewed and her next year as Queen of the garden begins.

The Mighty Ash by Julian Crooks

Alone, gaunt, spent and spare. The skeleton raises its arms to the heavens, scraping at the very clouds for a reprieve from the sentence of death. But it is too late – all life has fled or flown away. Winter begins to clothe the huge and proud old ash tree with its deathly shrouds. Passers-by look up and comment on the harsh beauty – the mighty figure has been conquered and stands stark and inert as a stone, a ghostly shadow of the incredible life-giving force that uplifted and sustained those creatures that lived in, on and around it just a few short weeks ago.

Although winter wants to mould with snow and ice a gravestone of this tree its wish will not be granted – at least not for long. For the ash's tough and rugged skin hides secrets deep within; the core is not so chilled as to be dead but merely dormant, waiting... And the slightest of tilts in the rotation of the earth triggers a barely perceptible reaction. Whilst its cousins, small and large, have woken from their slumbers and have been stretching out young leaves, the ash, the sleepiest of the woodland trees, responds at its own sloth-like pace. By the time of the spring solstice the progression of earlier dawns and later dusks has finally convinced the ash that now is the time for transformation. Charcoal conical buds that tip the twigs swell and magically begin to split and offer a shade of pond-scum green that hints at new life. Flinging forth its pale green compound, pinnate leaflets the giant announces its return. Passers-by glance up once more to marvel at the metamorphosis: the mighty ash has vanquished death and finally once more burst back into life.

An Oak by Steven Mitchell

My leaves brown and wither as you spend your days scampering around me, gathering fat acorns, which hang loose on my branches and lie fallen in the spaces between my exposed roots. As my shadow lengthens each day, you stuff your bounty into your winter stores, far more than you need, for when you get peckish.

*

Torn free by an icy north wind, the last of my leaves swirl across the meadow, some joining the wet mulch around my base. You, my russet friend, are snug in your drey, only venturing out when hungry, leaving me to survive the cold alone, morning frost on my boughs, every naked branch exposed to the whims of the weather. How I envy your fur coat.

*

The sun strengthens, pouring its nourishment on me, my branches tingling with budding leaves. Pale and tender, my leaves soon spread and darken to capture the fullness of the light. How grand I look? You scurry around, collecting twigs and feathers to cosy your drey in my broad, full canopy. I'm excited for the pups you trust me to shelter.

*

My roots heave water from deep underground to keep my leaves ripe and green, and in my shade, we remain cool from the brilliant sun. Your pups dance upon my branches, their tiny feet tickling my bark as they run up and down my broad trunk. You teach them I'm a friend and show them the acorns, small and green, which I'm growing for them. Like the acorns, they'll grow plump and strong and good.

The Generous Rowan by Sharon Williamson

As the year begins, the unassuming rowan at the end of the drive is grey and twiggy and bare, its branches used as a staging post to the bird feeders below. The remnants of last season's berries cling on, dried and shrivelled.

The days grow longer and the leaf buds start to swell, until a sudden burst of pale green clothes the branches. Blue tits chase each other through the delicate new leaves. The tree is soon covered in small white flowers and is full of insects, a feast for the finches and warblers that forage there.

Spring ticks into summer. The flowers fade to tiny green fruit, and the warm days turn the crop orange, then a brilliant red. The rowan in late summer is laden with bunches of bright berries, a magnet for all kinds of birds. As the days shorten the winter thrushes start to arrive, and they visit our driveway rowan in numbers.

But all too soon, it seems to me, the tree is stripped bare of its bounty; the leaves fall, and any berries that remain shrivel and dry in the cold winter winds, emergency rations for the hard days that may come.

It's not the tallest tree, or the prettiest or most graceful, but the generous rowan stands at the end of the drive like a sentry, waiting to welcome the annual cycle once more.

The Willow Tree by Sharon Linden

As the summer sun beats down, unrelentingly, my boughs sway under the weight of all and sundry basking under the cooling veil of my leafy, green canopy. Woodpecker hammers away at my elbow; I do wish he would be gentler. Over the fence, beneath the shelter of a bright blue parasol, lays a very dear old friend of mine, his faithful companion panting by his feet. With each passing year he slows. I only hope that the shade from my outstretched arms bring some added relief as he sleeps below.

This morning I awoke to a definite chill. Already a heavy sluggishness is setting in, not so much for my friend though. The diminishing heat has released him from his lethargy, and I hear him whistling below as he potters around his domain. Crisp, dried leaves swirl in the wind as he feeds his smouldering burner, always a tune from his lips. Oh, how his company cheers me!

Well, I hung onto my leaves for as long as I could, in the hope that winter would not arrive so swiftly, but now the earth, eerily silent, is swaddled in a blanket of white and there is no sign of my dear old friend. Every now and then, warm light gleams through a misted windowpane, and I hope he is inside warming his tired old bones. I could do with a warming myself.

The birds are singing, and when I awoke this morning, my branches were sprouting silky grey buds. Everything around me begins to awaken. Come on my friend, please be with us still. As the pale-yellow primrose begin to bloom, the first of this year's solitary bee drinks to its heart's content, frantically buzzing with delight at its sugary feast.

A creak…then a bark…and yes, here he comes, full of the joys of Spring!

A Year in the Life of a Crab Apple by Jenny Cooper

I lay in bed and see the top of the tree above the garden wall. A few unpruned branches have taken advantage of their freedom and reach towards the sky. A blackbird sits on the topmost tip to welcome the dawn with his morning song.

In spring the leaf buds burst into life, followed by clusters of small white flowers with pink tinged edges, that cover the tree like balls of cotton wool.

    Spring moves into summer, the petals fall to the ground like confetti and the fruits start to swell. Small hard green apples take the place of the flowers and mature as summer continues.

Heavy with fruit, the boughs bend downwards and soon a carpet of crab apples covers the ground beneath the tree.

    As the seasons change, the leaves fall and the skeleton is revealed against the blue sky.

    And still the blackbird sings his song.

GETTING HANDS ON IN NATURE

Introduction: Getting hands on in Nature

A large proportion of the tasks that students were asked to undertake on both courses involved them 'getting hands on' in the natural world, to interact and describe their experiences. These were the written sketches of the world that I enjoyed reading the most. It was wonderful to hear writers commenting that they couldn't believe how much they noticed on walks they had done hundreds of times – they simply had never really stopped to notice and observe.

When we look at the world with a fresh perspective, we can add a richness to our daily walks and interactions. We can also share the joy of our findings through our words.

It was pleasing to find that some writers also chose these tasks to reflect on childhood memories and experiencing nature with loved ones. The natural world can help us to maintain connection with our families and friends, particularly those that we have lost.
As adults we can forget to pause, to experience the world with wonder and delight. Exploring philosophy and nature we took time to learn about Forest Bathing and to enjoy the experience of being still. We are conditioned to always be active, always be 'doing'; when we go outdoors it is with an aim of getting somewhere, talking a walk or a run. Instead, we focused on the middle part of the experience, about stopping, and experiencing, about being

present rather than rushing to the next thing. I recommend you try this and I think you will find you will be surprised at what you notice that you haven't encountered before.

Part of the Exploring Nature Writing course asked the writers to consider what landscape meant to them. Landscapes are essential to provide a setting in many forms of writing, particularly in autobiography and memoir Landscapes form part of our identity and give rise to personal experiences shaping who we are from a young age. The work reflects the writer's journey into their past and also in relation to where they currently place themselves in the natural world.

A Walk Round an Urban Garden by Elizabeth Fairweather

There are baby birds and others chirping right and left as I step out of the doorway. The sun is warm on my face.

Pansies with mottled faces raise a smile. Fruit trees and shrubs bedecked with delicately scented white blossom. As the leaves grow, it makes it harder to pick out the birds.

Bright sunshine yellow dandelions with their jagged leaves have sprung up in the corner of the lawn. Food for the bees.

It seems the house sparrows are having a competition. There is one chattering to my right and another to my left.

Deep red wallflowers nod in the breeze.

Moving from the unyielding concrete area in the shelter of the house and on to the natural softness of the grass, the wind runs chill through my hair.

Daisies are springing up, and red dead nettle is in the lawn too. It isn't a perfect lawn, but I'd like to think it is good for wildlife. The daffodils are finishing now.

I become aware of a male Blackbird "socially distanced" away from me. He possibly thinks I have some food for him and his family? Brilliant. His presence brings a smile to my lips.

As I walk on, I realise there is more honesty than I thought, which hopefully should bring in some Orange Tip Butterflies when the weather is warmer.

I pause at the pond with its recently constructed seating area close by. The pond contains a striking marsh marigold with shiny yellow flowers, some of which I realise have five petals and others seven. There is a supersize green model frog watching over things near the edge.

Bird calls continue from all round.

The big conifer, planted by the previous owners of our house, dominates the area.

The birds are quick to make use of the fresh water I put in their bowl and a new suet cake.

Summer Loving by Nicky Hutchison

Slices of sunshine slant the copse

Bees fuzz and hum as

Drowsy flowers nod off.

A dandelion is brazen.

Trees sunbathe, crinkle and peel.

Dear yellow strokes my face to blush

I touch my warm cheek

And, just for a moment, I am loved again.

Yet by Nicky Hutchison

I try to breathe in time with the rise and fall of the ocean. I inhale as the wave gathers its smooth blue-green curve and we both sigh out as its effort crashes on the shore in a spent white froth that sets the glinting silver shingle thrilling and shivering as it draws in another breath. I cannot match its rhythm. I feel out of step. The sea's unceasing surge and swell, its roar and whisper makes me dizzy. There is wonder and panic in equal measure.

Salt-tanged squalls blow my hair to sandy strands which lash my face as if to bring me out of the dream. Leggy, speckled waders lope elegantly on the skirts of the sea like studious Victorian gentlemen searching for fossils, their hands clasped behind their back. Gulls glide overhead, veering wildly with the wind, laughing with joy and mocking the earthbound such as me. Their plaintive calls make me nostalgic for places I have never been, remind me that you have gone where I cannot follow. Yet.

Picnic at the Lighthouse by Steven Mitchell

Sitting at the base of the white lighthouse, sheltered from the sea breeze, I unwrap my limp sandwiches from their glinting silver foil. The grey waves breaking upon the shingle beach, teasing and jostling the stones with a gentle wash, mute the cries of gulls circling above.

   I look up the smooth, tall walls of the lighthouse to the clear sky, relieved the dark clouds threatening to spoil my adventure have vanished, having left only a few fat raindrops and a clean, salty scent in the air.

   A huge gull glides to land on the beach before me and pads around, titling its head, eyeing my sandwich, stepping closer. But this gull won't be getting any of my sandwich. The sea air has made me too hungry.

On the Beach by Sharon Williamson

I'm a Midlander, a child of land-locked counties. The sea is unfamiliar and exciting, an unexpected and longed-for pleasure. I breathe in the cool breeze; the sun and the wind is in my face as I sit looking out to the flat horizon, watching gulls, the unfamiliar tang of the shoreline fizzing my senses. Even the light is different. The familiar birdsong, the rustling of leaves, the rippling of grasses, the hum of traffic – all are absent in this new arena. It's immense, and it's an utter delight.

A Stormy Day by Sharon Williamson

Clouds race across the sky on a stormy day. All sensible creatures are hunkering down, out of the wind and rain, waiting for calmer weather. But as I watch, here's a thing – a trio of jackdaws hurl themselves skywards, chak-chak-chakking, blown and tattered by the unpredictable gusts, in playful delight in the turbulent air. A few minutes of glorious, giddying fun – a lesson for us all to grab such moments when we can.

Coastal Orchestra by Berenice Tregenna

The air has that fresh, pure scent of sea with its tinge of salt and fish filling my nostrils. My hair is whipped back by the wind and I inhale deeply. As I walk down the steps to the beach, I can hear the waves coming and going like the sea itself is breathing in and out. The sand shifts and crunches under foot as I make my mark, soon to be consumed by the tumbling water. I look down and it reminds me of demerara sugar ready to be mixed in my cake but this time bits of shell and small pebbles have been added instead of butter. Some of it is darker and already dampened by the pulsating surf. I can feel the moist droplets spray my cheek as I get closer to the breakers. A shadow of a sea gull flashes across as I hear its familiar call, another note in this coastal orchestra.

I Forgot my Swimming Costume by Nicky Hutchison

I set off for the woods dragging a nagging, fretful bag of worries. I was even anxious about the process of mindfulness. I do not do well at this. At the best of times, my thoughts scatter continuously like startled rabbits when they sniff a fox. It sometimes feels like being stalked by my own self. Being shaken on the shoulder just as you are nodding off into a reverie. 'Don't forget you have to do this, go there, be that someone, meet a deadline'. I was niggled too by the absence of a mobile phone. What if I needed to identify a bird on Chirpomatic? What if a photo opportunity presented itself and I had not got the camera?

The internal bickering continued until I reached the wood. There had been a murder. Six gleaming black crows fled at my approach. I knew I would find a body. A rabbit with a piteous brown leg stretched back, possibly in his final fatal escape effort touched me. The crows callously cronked, annoyed at the interruption to their feast. I continued through man-high bracken which seemed poised and self-assured and heard fuss and thunder as I put up a herd of deer although I never actually saw them, they were so well-camouflaged. Sudden encounters with wildlife never fails to thrill. My sense of smell is poor. But the air is clean and fresh, that much I know. When I put my nose to leaves and bracken, it is just a whiff of green, fleeting and all the more beautiful for that. I wonder at the perfume market, heavy laden scents exaggerated to a crass degree. How much more beguiling is a soft savour floating on a breeze. The stands of foxgloves look like forest sentinels of Summer. For the first time I look inside their pink bells and am amazed at the intricate spotting within. I can feel myself slowing after the dreaming drama of crows and deer.

    The air is not thick as I imagined it would be. It is light and for the first time I notice that the wood is primarily composed of silver birch. Long white trunks topped with numerous arrow head leaves, some new and soft green, others tougher, stiffer and darker. Their silver green canopy allows the sun to dapple the middle ground of the wood. The forest floor contains more shadows, hides more secrets.

    I sit on a crumbling stone wall. It is embraced by ivy who seems to be trying to hold together the remnants of man's folly to try to quarter and contain nature. In the distance the constant thrum of traffic reminds me the human impulse to be constantly moving forward. It is at odds with the now, here in the middle of the wood. Birch hugged by ivy, twining with oaks and the odd conifer. And, surprise, I am sitting under a robust rowan I had not noticed before. The trees stand waiting, strong and silent, enduring whilst we hustle our way to an early grave.

    It is nice to stop, to notice shade and the calm, kindly sunlight. To hear the shrill trill of small birds, the muted doo wop of a pigeon and the jeer of a crow. Just for a moment, I forget myself. Tears spring easily and I do not quite know why. I want to melt into the woods, float in the silence and simply be. Like the trees. But the traffic roars on.

Lost Connections by Rebecca Banks

Standing in a woodland, surrounded by the awe-inspiring grandeur of the canopy, it is worth taking a moment to consider what is underneath our feet. There is a labyrinthine mycorrhizal network. Millions of species of fungi and bacteria swap nutrients, transfer water, sustain connections, sustain life. These connections are essential for the health of this ecosystem.

The fungi involved in the 'wood wide web' as it is sometimes known, can be miniscule. Tiny. Almost insignificant. Yet together they can help prolong the life of a giant redwood or nurture new saplings.

So, the lesson is simple. Cherish the connections you do have and make new connections when you can.

To connect, is to live.

*In total 45% of adults report feeling lonely at some point according to the Campaign to End Loneliness

Holding My Breath by Julian Crooks

The firm sand cushioned the sole of each of my trainers. Like a welcome guest I sensed the privilege as I walked steadily, my footsteps, shadowed in the early morning sun, betraying my destination. Behind me oystercatchers piped peevishly and away to the left the screams of terns were carried on the salt-laden northerly breeze. Sand gave way to a line of sloping shingle, edged with cast up bladderwrack, dank and shrivelled.

Pebbles and rocklets, rounded and smooth were not as forgiving as the soft sand. My trainers were held, momentarily, as each one struggled for purchase and pressed down scrunching hard to ease me onwards towards the sea. After a few steps the crunch of the shingle and the cries of the birds were silenced by the water. Rolling crests laboured slowly towards the beach, crashed and dissipated shushing and dissolving.

I held my breath captivated by the aquatic pulse that beat time for me. And found myself breathing in time – waiting for the pause as the backwash rushed away out of reach, for that split second before it attacked once again. There it was! And in that minutest interval when the weight of water seems hung in freeze frame, undecided, uncertain, your heart, your very soul pauses too, halts suspended, waiting, anticipating, hoping, needing. And the truth is your conscious self does not recognise the infinitesimally temporary halt of the wave's retreat before it recommences its mighty surge as inexorable as the fall of a pendulum. Because you have become part of the wave and the wave has become part of you.

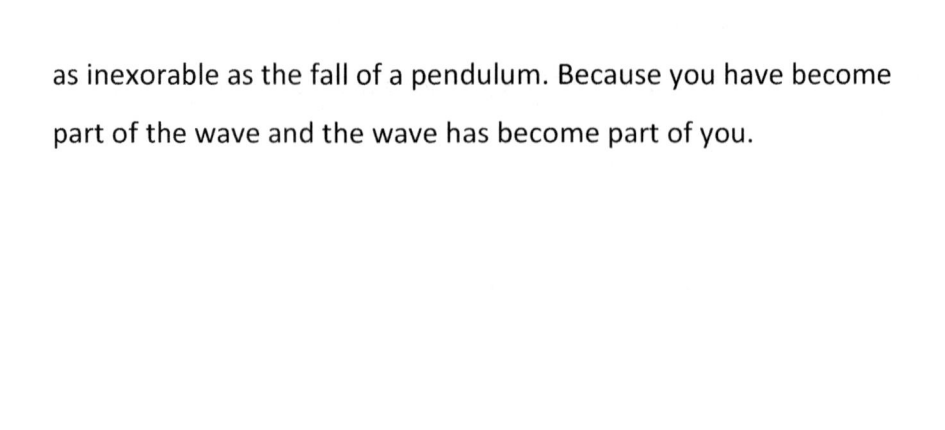

The Lane by Julian Crooks

I think it was the promise that was responsible for tempting me out and away from my comfy bed this Saturday morning; the promise of the Lane bereft of rat-run traffic; the promise of an hour alone with nature. You won't know my lane but it runs for a half-mile skirting the base of an escarpment, clothed in birch and heather, on its right before it reaches the main road. On the opposite side to the escarpment thick hedgerows with arable fields beyond draw your eye; the fields eventually dip down out of sight to the big river at the bottom of the valley.

The Lane is its own world. As you descend down the single carriageway road, shivering slightly in the chill east wind, the trees and hedges rise up around you enveloping you like a host of welcoming friends. Walk a little further and on that early spring morning the birdsong wraps around you from all sides: robins, blackbirds, blue and great tits, wrens, the occasional song thrush and at this time of year the newly arrived willow warblers, the occasional chiffchaff, blackcap and whitethroat, and, of course, the ever-present woodpigeon. A variety of calls and songs all proclaiming territory, but you wonder if they are simply calling out and singing to celebrate the warming of the earth and the expectation of a glorious spring day.

But it's also just become that time of year when the birds (despite their best attraction-seeking intentions) are difficult to spot. The birches, oaks, sycamores and sweet chestnuts have all responded to the annual tilting of the earth towards the sun. Delicate shoots and new-born leaves surge hopefully, clothing twigs and branches that only a week or two earlier were bare. Scan down from the treetops and you notice once more the brave blackthorn which has been blossoming brightly for weeks – a feast for the eye. Verges too are beginning to fill with patches of bluebells and here and there a startling mini galaxy of greater stitchwort. Amidst the understorey nettles and brambles are already well engaged in battle, squabbling for space in their battle for supremacy.

All of these distract and draw your vision, but the birdsong vies for your attention constantly: the strident, confident, repetitive call of the song thrush echoing across the valley, the plaintive, mournful but sweet descending call of the willow warblers, the sharp chak of the jackdaw and the most demanding of them all, a hyperactive and ignored child, the furiously energetic machine-gun rattle of the wren.

Halfway along and just past the copse is the newly seeded field. What do we have here? A pair of yellowhammers – the male in striking breeding plumage, a couple of mistle thrushes scanning the ground, perfectly camouflaged against the bare, dry earth, only their jaunty bounce revealing their presence. And then... yes, two hares! Forty metres away, unaware, lolloping lazily, sitting up on their haunches and now noticing me, turning and lolloping casually away.

An hour alone with nature – promise fulfilled.

Forest Bathing by Julian Crooks

The wood was peaceful that day. I discovered magic within it. Mid-May. Through the ancient gate the gently slope ascended to the wood stretched out on the hillside. The guardian of the wood huge and lightly-leafed stood impassive. I stroked his rough-ridged flanks and felt permanence, stability and endurance. How strange that something so dark-rutted and rugged should be so comforting. Beyond, the dappled sunshade, echoing with exotic nuthatch and excited chaffinch, beckoned me on.

It's often difficult being lost in the moment when you're a birdwatcher. Or, to be more accurate, a 'birdlistener'. For as the spring sun warms the earth, drawing up sap, shoots and stems the wood fills out with astonishing rapidity. An understorey of scrub and ancient flowering plants combines with the clothing of twigs and branches to offer shelter, nest sites and foraging opportunities to a host of wild things. Birds then are much more heard rather than seen. You expect to hear a call, perhaps, with luck, to see the caller. It was terribly hard to leave the binoculars, to leave the phone. These for me are integral tools on my quests for collecting, logging, confirming and counting.

And so, after a few minutes, I sat on a conveniently sited fallen trunk. I took in the moss and fungi on either side; grazed the moss with my palm; peered at the depths of hollies across the glade; gazed up at the cloud-scudding patches in the lofty canopy. This was nice. This was peaceful. I closed my eyes and let the soundscape take me over.

And then gradually it happened... my mind melted out of species recognition mode. It's not that I didn't acknowledge the identity of the blackcap or the great tit; I was in a state of inertia. The sounds of the wild things, the scents of plants and decay, the wood shared its secrets, had welcomed me in, and I was a part of it. Silent and still I may have been but not alone.

Hixbury Lane by Steven Mitchell

Stones crunch underfoot as I leave the tarmac onto the dirt track of Hixbury Lane. Sun passes through the blossoming blackthorn hedgerows bordering the path, dappling the ground with bright spots of light, and there's a fresh green perfume in the breeze. A cruising aeroplane leaves a fat vapour trail in the otherwise clear sky, and I wonder where it's heading to.

A few weeks ago, I walked here in wellingtons, slipping in mud and jumping puddles. Now, the earth is smooth and dry where the puddles lay, and ridged like mountains where boots sank deep in the mud.

A jay, dusky pink, with a blue flash on its shoulder, flits in an elder rising from the hedge, then lands before me on the path, snatching something up in its black beak before flying back between the leaves.

I greet a dog-walker coming along the track towards me, 'Nice day, isn't it?'

'Lovely,' she says, as her Labrador runs ahead.

Beside the track, dandelions, nettles and bluebells jostle under bramble. Two butterflies, one white, one yellow, flutter and dance above them. A bramble catches on my trousers and when I stop to unpick it, suddenly, a pigeon bursts from the hedge, tiny white petals scattering like confetti, floating and settling on the ground.

The lane slopes down, and curves right, banks of earth rising either side. And at the bottom, a thin, silvery trail of water crosses the track, escaped from a neighbouring field. I step into its flow to show it's welcome here.

River Walk by Sharon Williamson

I woke early, I remember. Really early. It was deep in the summer, and weeks into a heatwave. The bedroom was too warm already, and the promise of the cool of the morning was not to be ignored. I pulled on enough clothing to keep away any pre-dawn chill, and headed out on foot to the river.

My favourite walk is along the river, and it's a magical place in the summer. It's a slow, wide East Anglian waterway, banks thick with vegetation, with the occasional muddy slope where cattle gather to drink, standing knee deep in the cool water. Lily pads float in groups, damselflies dance and chase, and sometimes I spy a pike lurking in the weedy shallows.

This morning, though, was very special. All was still, and mist veiled the water, hiding the river from view. The quietness was astonishing. I picked my way along the footpath, trying not to break the spell. A sudden eruption from near my feet sent a shock of fright right through me – and I smiled in relief as I watched the pheasant flustering away. If he'd stayed put I would never have noticed him.

From the pre-dawn glow the sun rose through mist over the water. A moorhen called, and a heron flew lazily by. And slowly, slowly, the grey world of the night slipped away, and the day began.

Inspirations from the Sea by Sharon Linden

As I stretch out my hand, it leaves behind the itchy, woollen blanket beneath me, and finds itself nestled in a warm, dry, powdery nothingness. My fingers, enjoying this delight, delve deeper in exploration, hitting a firmer, colder layer harder to penetrate.

A loud shriek jolts me back to my senses as a larger-than-life gull glides overhead, eyes sweeping the barren ground for its next meal. In the distance, the gentle rhythmic lapping of water, pebbles hissing each time it retreats. From time to time a sudden surge, a more forceful crash, its bathers caught unawares.

I draw myself up and onto my feet, the ground sinking away and causing me to totter, like an infant taking its first steps. I steady myself, heading towards black jagged rocks erupting from the ground, all the while taking in the heady scent of wet vegetation and the smallest hint of salt on my lips.

Nearing the rocks, hidden in the hollows, I see a series of small pools each concealing many delights. If I were to lean down and dip my hand into its sun-warmed waters, I wonder what treasures I would find.

A Visit to Overhall Grove by Sharon Williamson

I walk along the bright, sunny footpath out of the village, into dense woodland. The day, which was already quiet, suddenly becomes even quieter; the air under the canopy is hushed, and the light filtering down is calm and green. No birds are calling. The atmosphere is soporific, and the scent of life and exuberant growth hangs heavy – I can almost taste the nettles that grow in thick beds. Elms and oaks thrust upwards from the green, and I pick my way along the narrow path towards a bank of bramble in a sunny clearing. Here butterflies dance, chasing and spiralling in the spotlight of sunshine, feasting on the bramble flowers. Back under the trees, no breezes stirs; every living thing is quiet on this hot day, and I am entranced.

The sharp bark of a muntjac jolts me awake from my reverie. I turn back towards the village, as a buzzard, unseen, calls overhead. The cool green woodland has washed me clean of the pressures of the day. As I emerge from the grove, I tell myself I will return, soon, for more of this peaceful remedy.

Hedgerow Bathing by Suzanne Thomas

My daily walk through the forest, the path is wide, the trees are small, this is the lane that goes past my house. I've often thought of it as a forest. There are some taller trees along the way, there is life in its thickets and clearings where gates lead to fields.

The Whispering Oak lives up to its name, greeting me as I stand beneath its branches, eager to hear my news. I am not silent on these walks, each thing that I see brings a response. I return the greeting to the tree, tell it what I'm doing and how things are.

The Dog Rose rambles through the hedgerow, pink petals unfurling among the tangle of green. There are so many plants here, so many fractals and patterns, my brain is loving it. Veins, stems, leaves and fronds.

The animals have been here too. The green tunnels heading towards a gap in the hedge, where muntjac, badger and hare squeeze through. Blackbird sings, the bumblebees forage, the ladybirds are busy, pale brown moths flitting as the sun goes down.

I notice everything, or it feels like it. The worries of the day pushed aside, I can breathe again. I smile as I walk home, gently touching grasses and leaves as I pass, feeling part of it all.

Into the Forest by Katie Lloyd

Walking through knee-high grasses and cushions of yellow birds-foot-trefoil, I approach the woodland edge. With every moth that flutters and grasshopper that springs from the grassland, thoughts of emails and to-do lists gradually lift from the forefront of my mind. Through the gate I step into the warm, still shade of the forest. I'm reminded of the times I would crawl into my makeshift tent as a child. Made with bedsheets and strategically placed chairs, I would take a book and it would be my world for a moment.

    I walk along a narrow path, edged with ferns and hip-high sedges, feeling the dust-dry ground through my boots. The repertoire of a distant song thrush echoes and a nearby blackbird rattles an alarm call as it scrambles and flies from beneath bramble.

    I feel my shoulders loosen and my breath deepen. The clouds move and sunlight drops through the canopy, flooding the floor with a depth of colour and shade. My eyes take it in, a welcome rest from the strain of screen-staring. Two chiffchaffs start up either side of me, competing in their seesaw song.

    I lean against an oak tree, feeling its rough bark catch on my top. Barely-there craneflies dance through shafts of sunlight. The warmth of the leaf-littered ground fills the air with a dry, sweet earthy smell. I breathe it in. Overhead, a woodpecker drums.

GETTING HANDS ON IN NATURE-HUMAN CONNECTION

Sandcastles by Elizabeth Fairweather

A little girl on the beach with Mum and Dad

Built a castle tall with

bucket after bucket of sand.

Pebbles and shells

formed windows and doors.

Finally, a moat round the castle edge.

More digging and a tiny stream

linked the castle to the sea.

Time brought the tide along.

A trickle at first.

Seeping into our memory.

Dens by Steven Mitchell

In the wood behind our house,

My brother and I build dens.

Wigwams of fallen sticks propped against trunks.

Dried grass for walls.

Dirt floor swept bare.

Then we sit, bored in the shade

Until Mum calls us for our tea,

And we talk of badgers enjoying the home we've built for them.

Feeding the Ducks by Nicky Hutchison

Chubby fingers throttle the twisted neck

of the plastic bag of white bread.

At the pond there are no ducks,

just the swampy ribbons of mermaid's hair

sway beneath the surface as the pond laps.

We crane our necks to the reeds and flag.

Then, the mallard armadas muster.

An arrow of olive ducklings sails into our port.

They mill around mis-thrown morsels.

Quick and perfect.

At the last regretful snowfall of bag crumbs

the fluffy flotilla sails back into open water,

their speckled brown squadron leader

honking orders for the next mission.

Memory Trees by Hilary Park

Our childhood ran from tree to tree.

Two wise oaks held us safe.

race there to the Two Top Trees,

circle the furrowed trunks,

round their tortoise roots

tyres softening. But not beyond.

We dashed the laburnum by,

its yellow chains flickering

idly, threatening to froth us

at the mouth. Past the sparrowed

pines, ink green and fragrant

to the dell of our garden

place. Earth scooped low we lay

hammocked in the half light,

swaying under boughs,

breathing in apple and land and summer.

Making plans until my mother's voice.

Sang out,

miles away – drawing us in.

Then running past the rainbow sumac,

past the dragon bonfire warm

into the kernel of her house.

The Laburnum by Sharon Linden

At the bottom of the garden sits a portal, where the sun enters this world. High above, on a broad wooden pedestal it sits, dangling its sunbeams from every branch, tantalisingly close to my head. I am sure I could catch one if I tried.

With arms and legs not equal to the task, but with reckless determination, I do battle with its smooth but knotted trunk, each advance leaving grazes on my skin. I must not give in; my time is short as dusk quickly approaches. With one final push I leap upwards, then open my eyes, dazed, as I lay on the damp earth below.

I sit myself up then stand, head hung low. How I wish I could hold a sunbeam.

Slowly I begin to rise, two strong arms lifting from behind, and I tuck myself firmly into the immovable fork of its branches. My hand quivers and the tears dry as the tips of my fingers make contact with a silky, golden beam of light, and my little heart bursts with joy.

A Natural Christmas Present by Elizabeth Fairweather

We stood a foot or so from the edge of the expansive, grey sea and felt our skin tingle as thousands of Pink-footed Geese exploded out of the water.

The birds flew towards us in straggly skeins, filling the sky above us. Their contact calls rang in the chilly morning air. We heard the sound of their wingbeats as they ventured over our heads, en route to their favourite feeding spots in the fields in the surrounding countryside.

The waves lapped softly back and forth on the edge of the tidal mudflats, leaving just the shingle and various plants. The occasional wave was tipped with white as the high tide receded.

Other birds – waders and ducks – had been driven from where they had been feeding on the mudflats as the tide had swept in, temporarily covering their meal table. They had taken refuge in the lagoons behind the hides at the Snettisham RSPB reserve.

A brilliant, memorable way to start a Boxing Day morning.

A Morning Dog Walk by Nicky Hutchison

A dawn breeze clasps my cheeks in a chill embrace as a quiet green riot goes on in the verge. Spearheads, waxy spatulas and straps jostle for position with jagged nettles whilst gentle white stars of chickweed and leggy cow parsley stand impassive in the hushed furore. Brassy yellow daffodils, the warm up act for the real show, are giving way to more understated natural hues: dog violets laying low, shy cream comfrey chimes hang their heads, silver stars of wild garlic gape heavenwards from smooth lush foliage whilst metallic bluebells dissolve to mist en masse.

Meanwhile, the sun is waking. The horizon is a peachy beige leaching to white then skyward to duck-egg blue, silhouetting trees cut out by winter but their stark edges now softened by spring buds. Opposite, the moon plays a last game of hide and seek between houses and trees before fleeing the morning.

There is a subtle gap in the hedge where the new sun stretches and shimmers. It is framed by two guardian oaks. The left-hand oak points a strong finger north whilst his right-hand brother throws an arm with a stern warning to go south. Anywhere but due east, into the sun. There's a pull of magic about the gapway that is hard to resist.

But we go North, up the path to the woods where the avian orchestra is tuning up from the jungle of beech, holly and hawthorn. An endless chirrup of bird gossip cheers us on. A graceful group of eleven deer in the neighbouring field take our measure then take off as one, under unseen direction. A rabbit scarpers out of sight. Beech, holly and oak and sifting sunlight give way to a sombre conifer plantation, the long straight trunks implacable in the silence holding their dark secret close, so we hurry along the dried, dusty path back into the light lanes where dark ivy cascades over dry stone walls, smothered by her jealous grip. Bare rough stone is age-spotted white with lichen or coated in a close-cut golden brown beard of moss. Ivy is busy elsewhere. She crawls up the trunk of an oak and although she cannot reach his arms, she holds his torso tight in a ravishing grip, like a dangerous, needy lover.

On the green, creamy cherry blossom is ready for a lavish wedding casting a delicate buttery scent and confetti strewn on the grass as if we have just missed the ceremony.

There are no starlings today. They are usually strung on the telephone wires, like black notes on a stave for a Summer sing-a-long, but all I can hear is the mocking laugh of a crow and the distant doodle of a cockerel. The morning has begun in earnest.

Pine Cone by Steven Mitchell

My toddler son passes me you in his warm palm and says, 'For you, Daddy.'

You are almost weightless as I bounce you in my hand; surprising, as you grew and fell from the colossal pine casting its shadow on us.

Egg-shaped and tawny, rough and dry. I hold you to my eye and smile, noting that each scale of your intricate body looks strangely like a pair of parched and puckered lips.

'Look. It's open,' I say, showing my son the shady spaces between the segments. 'That means it's going to be a nice day.'

The Official Water Collector by Rebecca Banks

My little fingers are clasped tightly around the handle of my bright red bucket. I run from where my sister is bossily creating our sandcastle masterpiece. I know my job. I am the official water collector in our construction duo. This is an important job, where only brave six-year-olds will succeed. Our moat needs water, and I am determined to fulfil this mission. As I run, my small footprints hardly mark the sea-saturated sand, little heel indents where water briefly pools. In my haste, I catch my toe on a scrappy shell and hop for a moment, before courageously carrying on. My arms pump lightly, taking me onwards, towards the shore. The rhythmic roar of the waves drowns out my determined breathing and as I get closer to the water, the sea-spray lands on my round freckled face. And I pause.

    I look at the water and I am scared of the immense space. The overwhelming sound of the waves fills my ears, and I am scared and exhilarated by the power and mystery of the sea.
Stepping forward, I lower my bucket. My feet creep forward, and I gasp at the pins and needles cold that consumes my little legs. My sharp breath is full of fresh, salty air and I briefly wonder if this is what seaweed tastes like? My bucket scoops and I turn and run before the next wave chases me back towards my sister.

I proudly present my half-filled bucket and together we solemnly tip it into the moat, where is instantly seeps into the sand below and disappears.

My sister nods and I am off again.

I am the official water collector.

But I might need a bigger bucket.

My Granny's Pond by Rebecca Banks

I am squatting,

Feet flat against the mossy mosaic of paving slabs,

Concealed by the huge hydrangea bush, so good for hide and seek.

Snippets of adult-babble and birdsong mingle in the breeze.

Scents of Spring and roasted Sunday lamb waft towards the pond.

Mesmerized by the bubbles of life beneath the surface,

My fingers tickle the cool water,

Gently scooping,

To catch a tiny frog, no bigger than my fingertip.

He is squatting,

Feet flat against my skin,

And we consider one another,

For just a moment.

Freewheeling on Cannock Chase by Rebecca Banks

I am face down, my body strewn across the mossy embankment, my hands covered in mud, the taste of dirt on my tongue.

We cycled these routes so often. Getting up early on Saturday mornings, heading off before breakfast, we would ride for hours it seemed, as the sun's soft rays fought through the clouds, to be rewarded with an alfresco picnic breakfast (a bowl of cornflakes) eaten from the comfort of the boot of the car.

It had been spectacular. A free-wheeling, body-flipping somersault of a fall. I had been earnestly trying to keep pace with my sister and Dad. Yet I was trailing behind, and the dark whispers of the dense forest tickled my spine. What lurked within these woods? I had heard tales that black panthers roamed the Chase. And my mind took me to the brownies and goblins of Blyton's tales. So, I pushed a little harder, feeling every stone and crevice as I picked up speed, the bottle-green pine trees blurring. It was exhilarating, flying along, on the cusp of losing control.

But their bikes were superior to mine. They had gears. My little pink bike had only a comical hooter, which I pressed every so often to provide an encouraging honk, like a goose in flight. Yet I didn't even have chance to sound this alarm, before my front wheel dipped and I careered over the handlebars and into the wayside. Thick fronds of bracken reached to catch me, their verdant scent filling my mouth, as I let out a small cry. The momentary ringing in my ears drowned out the agitated 'chink, chink, chink' of a blackbird interrupted.

I am face down and my tears fall. A droplet of blood percolates the earth.

I am part of this forest.

Childhood Landscape by Charlotte Dale

My carefree childhood – a magical garden divided into sections; two yards with brick outhouses full of spiders, veg patch full of worms, lawn with two pure white grazing geese and my favourite – a brook. Days spent wearing my much-loved corduroy trousers with elastic waist. As I pulled my wellington boots over thick socks, I couldn't wait to get into the brook. To the soundtrack of honking geese I'd let cold water flow over my wellies, searching for my most valuable find – tadpoles. Grabbing at their dark oval bodies with frantic swimming tails, I'd put them in a dish to have a closer look, not quite getting my head round that one day they would be a frog.

After dry spells and the 'wrong' time of year when no tadpoles could be found, I'd turn my attention to the fragments of man-made debris. A bottle top here, a marble there but my favourite was pottery. I'd stick my small fingers into squelching clay mud and I'd pull out triangular bits of broken pottery, buffed edges from years of running water. Overjoyed when I'd find a pattern other than blue-and-white willow. Who broke those plates? How did they get there? I collected the pieces, storing them, convinced that one day I could piece them altogether like a ceramic jigsaw. Only when the dusk chorus sang, or my toes would be numb from the cold and the geese were locked up, did I then go into the house.

In the Churchyard by Rebecca Banks

The wrought iron gate creaks a welcome, as I enter the churchyard with my dog Charlie. I follow the path, pitted with holes and crevices, aged and careworn after so many years of shepherding people around the grounds. On the left there is a wild area, buzzing with life. The brown, crinkled petals of the daffodils hang onto their final moments, whilst the pastel primroses emerge, peeking sleepily through the undergrowth. It is quiet and peaceful. I walk beneath the inky-green shade of the yew tree and breathe in the damp, mossy perfume. The calm is broken by the harsh caw of the crows building nests in the rafters of the church. Surrounded by grey, crumbling gravestones, they are busy bringing in new life. I walk a little further, past the cherry tree, heavy with blossom. As the breeze whispers, my face is showered with baby pink confetti, like a bride.

The sun emerges, casting stippled light through the branches of the beech tree. The Japanese have a wonderful term for these streaks of sunlight hitting the earth from the heavens; 'komorebi'. For me, in that moment, I shall simply call it hope...

A Haven Revisited by Sharon Linden

A babbling stream twists and turns beyond an old stone bungalow, nestled on the edge of a farm. A temporary home, many moons ago, a haven and escape from the cold grey of a concrete world, and from problems too large to surmount.

The glistening waters wend their way through field after field and I see myself from yesteryear, walking companionably along beside it. As it travels, it gently draws up the troubles deep within me and carries them away, far beyond the old stone bridge.

I arrive at last at an aging, slatted walkway, a place of temporary tranquillity. There I sit, both legs dangling, barely above the swirling waters below. I raise my face, eyes closed, soaking up the warmth and breathing deeply the clean, fresh air, immune now to the pungent aroma which accompanies a farm.

From behind me a mother ewe, alert to my presence, frantically calls her new-born to safety, one beady eye warning me not to approach. The cows low in yonder fields; finally, my companion arrives.

With a sudden, loud crow and a great clamour in an overgrown bush, my pheasant friend alights, and there we sit, and I open my heart while he nods his head and blinks one eye, the weight steadily lifting.

Slowly now, the scene dissolves away before my eyes, and there I am left standing, forever thankful that nature's healing powers have worked their magic on me.

July 1972 by Julian Crooks

From the car park where the minibus had dropped us off it was a short but steep walk down the valley to the beach. Sultry air enclosed by the scrub-covered valley sides alive with familiar robins, blackbirds, dunnocks, tits and wrens jubilant on this July mid-morning, but exotic cries of warblers (unknown to us then) that surely didn't belong in England.

Suddenly the valley was behind us and the bay opened out in front. The salt-filled breeze was cool and welcome. The chalk cliffs to either side collected the light and threw it back at us, mischievously daring us to gaze with non-squinting eyes. Treading gingerly over lumps of rounded chalk we tentatively made our way to the sea… and stared. Transfixed by the ever-changing movement of the surface, the sun-dappled shadows shifting on the sandy bottom and the gently rhythmic slap and shush of each wave.

The beach swept round in a crescent to left and right, backed by the turf-topped chalk cliffs. Amazingly, we were on our own, a couple of boats on the horizon the only evidence of human existence. The bay held us in its warm, encircling embrace and glancing shyly at each other, catching each other's eye like explorers in a new found land, we acknowledged our unexpected bond. The vista before us was unlike anything we had seen or experienced before; it was technicolour and panoramic and (for this precious moment at least) it was ours.

Egged on by the cries of gulls and our innate, young curiosity we began our journey to the headland.

That Robin's Back Again by Julian Crooks

I did not develop an interest in nature through my parents – they had no especial interest in the natural world beyond enjoying some scenery and nice weather. Very occasionally though one of them would drop the odd comment that, for me at least, very young and impressionable, had a greater and longer lasting significance than they might have imagined. The house in which I grew up in as a child was small with modest, narrow pockets of 'garden' front and back. It did not seem like much of a haven for wildlife. But winters were something of an exception; whenever a hard frost settled or snow fell, garden birds largely absent for much of the year suddenly became plentiful, tempted by slices of bread torn into small chunks. Cue my father's casual aside: 'That robin's back again!' And so he was – puffed up, perched atop a privet hedge looking at us in a manner suggesting he was just as interested in us as we were in him.

My dad's casual comment hid, I believe, a sense of satisfaction and even validation – here was an old friend who had chosen to return to our garden. We hadn't seen him for the best part of a year and, of all the gardens he could have chosen he had selected ours. Subconsciously for my dad (and me in my innocent youth) it was akin to seeing the return of a family member. I'm certain that the robin's appearance was not a consequence of sentimental longing on its part; no, unlike most birds that might visit the garden and fly off as soon as you are seen at the window, the robin will remain, peering back at you inquisitively, inviting an unspoken dialogue. Much folklore exists around robins largely focussing on the belief that it is a friend to humans and even sacred (one myth suggests that it was originally brown and gained its red breast after drops of Christ's blood fell on it from the cross). It's no surprise then to learn that it is considered bad luck to kill a robin.

It was quite a few years later as a committed wildlife enthusiast with a thirst for knowledge that I realised my dad had been labouring under a misapprehension. The lifespan of a British robin is often less than two years. Sadly, the robin which my dad had been welcoming back to our garden each winter was unlikely to be the same bird year on year. It is with a pang of regret that I confess that, as a clever clogs teenager, I put my dad right on this point. He would have none of it. This cheeky chappie, fluffed up, braving the bitter winds of winter was definitely the same bird – it perched on exactly the same twigs each year, held your gaze and uttered that wistful, liquid trickle of honeyed notes in the same way each year. How could it not be the same bird?

A World of my Own by Sharon Linden

Through a hidden gate at the end of the garden I enter a secret world. Behind me, people, noise and clamour but I bid them farewell and make my escape, instead, to a land of wonder.

Where shall we go today? Should we travel this secret realm, or sit at its entrance and drink in its wonders?

Slowly, descending makeshift steps cut into an old embankment, wrestling my way past a wiry willow determined to embrace after a long, solitary winter, I decide to just sit on the very last step and drink in the beauty of this now-awakening world. Taking a slow, deep breath I open my eyes… and connect.

Rising high behind me, last year's creepers scale the side of the banking, and the last of Springtime's daffodils push their golden trumpets through the decaying latticework. At my feet lays a worn and dusty path, where railway lines once ran. Old wood, fallen from trees, lay scattered about like gnarled and dry old bones.

In the distance a great tit sings, sounding like a rusty hacksaw determined to finish its work, and a woodpigeon begins his muffled, husky call but is cut off mid coo.

Long-departed willow herb still stands, proud and upright along the way, swaying gently in the breeze and behind it, the old wood of hawthorn, gradually receding behind fresh green ruffles of new life.

Flitter, flitter, a tiny bird bobs up and down towards me, but no, something isn't as it should be, so he turns and flees into the woods.

I flick away an inquisitive fly and my eye falls on the only thing here that brings me grief, a plastic bottle, one of many along this path. Oh, if only people understood!

Gently, a catkin from the willow overhead floats down and brushes my shoulder, drawing me back to the beauty around me. A much better place to be.

Clouds are drawing overhead, rain is sure to come, to nourish the life around me and to soothe me another day. Time to take shelter, but I'd gladly stay and be soaked through than leave this world behind.

From Here to There – North Pennines by Hilary Park

We drive across the moor, watching the landscape smudge at the edges where the distant solway promises sea. The heathland knits into the moss – into the blanket bog which makes the peat that works the wilderness for us. Should we stop and walk I know the woven hues would soft creak and gently give beneath my boots. The air would clean my mind of thoughts and cotton grass would catch the pale light. But we drive on – turning fast, the wide sky meets the curve of the road and my heart freefall floats as lapwings tumble an iridescent sheen then safe and away. Soon we will reach the place where silent woodland glens give dreaming shadow space to siskin and russet deer.

The mountains will cluster near in blued swathes of spring, where the beck is running and the creatures thrive.

Seaview by Sarah Carlin

When I am here, I feel that time is standing still, and yet I am reminded of our insignificance, as we pale away against the sea's magnificence.

The Martello Towers look like far off ghostly ocean-liners, a throw-back from another age. Massive sky. Salty spies.
The clouds are like shapeshifters, chameleons, never quite one thing nor another, but they hold me captivated by their endless dance.

I walk down to the water, gingerly picking over the stones that feel cool and jagged under my feet. On the shifting sands, my footprints softly imprint and then disappear. The stinking seaweed, dried up like ancient mummies, is pungent and petrified.
On the surface, the waves seem so gentle, yet underneath I know the waters are teaming with life. Where land meets the sea, you get the sense of the everlasting circle of life – an ouroboros.

Gulls like Sopwith Camels are waiting to attack, their incessant cries pull my gaze upwards.

The wind puffs in my face, "Blows away the cobwebs..." my Dad's voice surfaces from my memory. His body has now gone, but his spirit remains and always visits me here.
My son's melodic laughter floats, muffled from the distance, then he runs to meet me by the shore.

FICTION WRITING

Introduction: Fiction Writing

At the start of this anthology, I described the way that the courses had been designed to teach sketching with words, with the aim of building up observations of the natural world, not only as an aid to connecting more deeply with nature, but also as a way of building up rich resources of words and phrases that can be used in larger pieces of work.

In Developing Nature Writing we explored how to connect with nature through art, philosophy, and folklore, alongside learning about general fiction writing. This chapter contains work from the following themes of writing:

General Fiction Writing: In this section you will find work written around using natural landscapes as a background for interactions.

Writing inspired by Art: Writers were asked to choose a favourite piece of art and imagine that they were standing next to the painter as the painting was being created. This technique enabled the writers to immerse themselves in nature through other artists' eyes. It also helped us to understand how we ourselves are painting with words when we bring together the images that form a story in a piece of writing.

Folklore: I used popular folklore as a start point to exploring mythology linked to the natural world and developed it further reimagining traditional tales, as well as creating our own stories linked to species of plants and natural finds such as hagstones that have folklore and mythology attached to them.

Science Fiction Writing: In our final section we took the idea of our natural world on planet earth and considered what plant species we would take with us to another planet.

The Lock by Patricia Martin

Early one morning as the sun's rays tint the stone of Dedham church tower, a lighterman struggles to open the heavy lock gates on the River Stour. His cargo of barley filling the body of the lighter is on its way to Mistley Wharf to meet the seagoing Thames barges and thence to London, to return in two days time with iron, coal or oil to heat and light Suffolk.

The lock is built of great sides of oak, the river water giving no way to the efforts of the man as he kneels to give extra purchase to his efforts. Only a five foot drop of water is demanded by the workings of the mill, but it is maybe a two-man task to fill the lock for the boat to pass.

Across the fields towards Dedham hares glow golden in the thin early rays of sunlight and the swallows, swooping low to catch the first flies and midges, call their twittering trill to each other. Slowly the lock fills with river water, the gates ease open and the lighter is poled through, the wooden hull creaking as it continues its steady, unhurried journey towards the sea.

Misty Lake by Kate Stacey

Early one morning she slipped out of the house, took her bicycle from the wall, and tiptoed along the side path and out of the gate. She pedalled off down the silent street with the curtains drawn across the windows like closed eyes, rapidly leaving the town behind as she headed into the countryside. She would be at the lake before the town started stirring.

    The water was flat calm, a mirror reflecting the grey clouds, but there was a low mist blurring the far shore. She pedalled on, down a quiet lane, heading for a little stony beach below a bluff with trees and bushes that would hide her from view. When she reached the beach and stood at the edge of the water, the stillness made her hold her breath. The mist cloaked the view up the lake and muffled any sounds from across the water. She felt like she was in her own soft grey cocoon.

    She stepped slowly into the water, careful not to splash and disturb the peace or give her presence away. Gentle ripples spread out in concentric rings from her feet, breaking the reflections. She reached the point where she could float and watch the swells of water moving away from her. She didn't dare to swim and disturb the water even more. Suddenly something leapt vertically out of the water in front of her and her heart leapt into her mouth. It was so quick that she couldn't see what it was, just a plop as it landed back in the water creating rings of water spreading towards her. She watched the fish's ripples meet hers and create a cross hatch of little ridges. Gently she took her first stroke, keeping her arms below the surface and letting her legs droop to avoid any splashes. The water formed a swell in front of her as she swam, as if she was pushing the water forwards, and became a series of ever decreasing waves. Except they were barely waves, just raises in the surface that slowly dissipated as she passed. There was a pale grey silveryness to the tops of the ripples reflecting the clouds and the light. It was like swimming in liquid silver or mercury and the laziness of the water's movement suggested a thicker more viscous liquid than she could feel with her hands and her body. Below the surface the water felt silky and smooth, flowing along her sides like silk.

The hills on either side of the lake rose above the mist as she got further away from the shore. They too were grey and blurred at the edges in the soft early morning light. The mist on the lake would burn off as the sun got high. The hills would become sharp outlines in the sun and noise and people would shake everything awake. Just for now though, it was a soft sleeping pale grey world, inside her own cloud.

The Lily Ponds and the Bumblebee by Patricia Martin

'The best feature of the gardens are the lily ponds. You will find them along the path, past the rose gardens.' The lady in the kiosk at the entrance of the National Trust gardens smiled at the boys and handed their mother a leaflet showing a map of the grounds. 'Frogs live in lily ponds' said Robin aged 4 and raised on Beatrix Potter so knew about these things, 'with fishing rods.' He hurried after his brother Alex, 7, who was already making his way quickly through the rose garden, ignoring the voluptuous scents and colours.

'Are there fish? I can see fish, look look, and a dragon fly and another!'

'I think the blue ones are damsel flies' said Mum, 'and see the stream between the ponds – that is called a rill, and the big leaves each side are hostas.'

'Oh there is a Monet bridge' said Mum. The boys did not know what a Monet was, but the bridge might be good for Pooh sticks, if the water was not covered by lily pads with red, white and yellow flowers. 'The yellow ones are the best,' said Robin. 'The frog likes them best.'

The sky darkened and heavy drops of a sharp summer rainstorm fell across the garden. The dragonflies disappeared beneath the hosta leaves and the boys put the hoods of their jackets over their heads.

'I've found a bumble bee on the grass– but it's still, it's not moving. Is it dead?'

'It looks dead. Shall we bury it?'

'I think we should have a funeral Mum'

'Perhaps, but there are ice creams for sale in 'The Olde Tool Shed' so shall we go there first? We are getting rather wet at the moment.'

'So's the bumble bee.'

The Walled Garden by Sharon Williamson

It was late afternoon by the time we arrived, stiff-limbed and tetchy from the long drive. We dumped our bags in the hallway of the rented cottage and headed straight out to the garden to stretch our legs and reclaim some kind of calm for ourselves. Bliss. It was bliss just to stand there and feel the breeze, faces upturned into dappled sunshine, tense shoulders melting back to a semblance of normality. That's what being outside can do.

A wren suddenly exploded into loud song nearby, shaking me back to the present moment. Looking around, I noticed a gate set into the red-bricked wall on the far side of the lawn. I remembered mention of 'large gardens' in the description when I'd made the last-minute booking. We decided to investigate.

We followed the path around the lawn and came to the gate, which was held closed only by a heavy latch. On the other side we found a small slice of perfection. It was a walled garden, a little overgrown perhaps, but fragrant and bursting with promise. An espalier fig was splayed along a sunny wall, soaking up the warmth like a sun-seeking holidaymaker. Flower beds and fruit bushes held all sorts of treasures, and, best of all, there was a large pond, into which a frog plopped, alarmed at our approach.

I smiled. This was perfect.

Garden Date (a very short story) by Charlotte Dale

I don't know why we decided to come here for a first date; it wasn't the usual sort of place. I took my jacket off and wiped my brow, we'd only just set foot in the hothouse and already I was feeling the heavy damp atmosphere. Huge palms reached towards the dome glass roof, like green hands reaching for the sun. A tropical butterfly flew past, slowly showing off the lime green upper wings with iridescent eyes. Not darting and fluttering like the native butterflies I'd just witnessed in the wildflower meadow. No, this was unhurried and leisurely. It landed upon a light green leaf which highlighted its beauty even further – making sure I'd seen its splendour. As we meandered our way through the narrow path the silence was comfortable. We drank in the vegetation of foreign lands and as I looked ahead something caught my eye from outside – giant lily pads.

On exiting the glasshouse I noticed my reflection – frizzy hair. He hadn't seemed to notice and we were both absorbed in the calmness of nature. On looking at the giant lily pads, I had the urge to do a childlike run, hop, skip and jump across them to reach the other side of the lake, using them like steppingstones.
"I've just got the urge to sit in one of those huge lily pads," he said. I smiled. I think we're a good match and it was a good place for a first date.

Writing Inspired by the Film 'Kes' by Julian Crooks

Early one morning he stepped over the stile, carefully avoiding the nettle spears which thrust up to assault him on either side. Mid-June. The breeze had picked up and as he followed the path along the field edge he felt as though he was walking the shoreline of a strange green sea; the yard-high barley was a benign green sea lapping at his arm. The drystone wall to his left, blackened by decades of colliery dust was greened and brightened now with red campion, buttercup, sheep's sorrel and, at intervals, purple foxgloves, erect as guardsmen at their sentry posts. The noise of traffic from the village was behind him and he caught the urgent, sweet rattling of a skylark floating down to him.

In the distance the clank of the winding gear was echoed by a pair of boisterous, humbug-patterned magpies intent on mischief. It was hard to believe that a few hundred yards below this path, these fields, his father, brother and hundreds of other men were toiling in near darkness, their nostrils and mouths filling with coal dust as they heaved their picks and shovels.

Five minutes later and over the crest of the hill it loomed like some monstrous machine scouring the earth to plunder its riches. Like some nightmare vision sent to despoil Paradise the pithead and giant winding wheel towered stark and alone. A satanic piece of Meccano, yet a part of this green and pleasant land.

A Lost World by Kate Stacey

I looked at the black blank windows of the house as I drove towards it and wondered why they looked so foreboding. Despite passing the house regularly, it never felt any friendlier. I'd asked my neighbours about it not long after moving to the village but their answers showed indifference. It had been built a long time ago and had been empty longer than anyone could remember. No-one seemed to know who had owned it or who it belonged to now. It felt abandoned, as if something dreadful had happened there that the village had deliberately forgotten. Even on a sunny day, it felt forlorn, the big windows in the facade like dark eyes looking out onto the lake.

It must have been the owner's crowning glory when it was built. It had such a presence, a statement of wealth and fashion, with the pillars of pale sandstone facing the road so that you couldn't fail to take notice as you approached. I slowed and pulled the car onto the grass verge and looked again. I wanted to walk around the building and appreciate its beauty and presence, though I didn't think I would be brave enough to look in the windows. "Well, why not?" I got out of the car. I found myself almost tiptoeing on to the terrace under the portico. It was such a grand classical building. The huge columns towered above me and the underside of the portico was carved with floral details. The lake below was framed between the pillars. Someone had thought about how this view would look.

Now that I was closer, and not driving, I could see that the lake curved around the side of the house. "In for a penny..." I stepped off the terrace and into a wild meadow. The vegetation reached to my thighs and the air hummed with insects as I pushed my way through. I was making a trail and, feeling slightly guilty, glanced at the house but there were fewer windows on this side, and they didn't look as unfriendly as the ones at the front. I waded on through the sea of grass and flowers, admiring the rippling beauty and the many colours dotted through the greens. This must have been a manicured lawn when the house was occupied. Probably the pride and joy of the owner – and never ceasing work for the gardeners, who wouldn't have had a sit on mower to help them. I ought to be careful in case there was a ha-ha hidden in the grass. Ahead a line of mature dark trees marked the end of the meadow, and under their shade the vegetation became lower. I waded carefully towards them, watching the ground for hidden features, until I reached the dappled light of woodland, pausing for a moment to let my eyes adjust. There was grass seed all over my trousers. Ahead a faint path wound between the trees, and I followed it. The trees, like the columns of the house, towered over me. They were huge specimens, mature and magnificent, probably collected as seeds on someone's grand tour and brought back to be planted, though that lost person would never have seen them like this. A garden on this scale, a landscape really, must have had a huge team of gardeners. Just as I thought this, I glimpsed a high red brick wall between the trees. A walled garden? The path led on towards it and now I could see an old wooden gate in an arch in the brick. And there, sitting regally and serenely as if waiting for me, was a beautiful black cat.

I stopped. I hadn't expected to meet anything, or anyone, though to be honest I hadn't thought about that when I stepped out of the car. The cat didn't move or blink, just sat upright and looked at me with typical cat aloofness. I suppose a cat could live in this garden, there would be enough birds and mice for it to survive, but it didn't look feral. Its fur was shiny and smooth, and it looked far too proud. As if reading my mind, the cat stood up and turned to walk slowly into the garden, holding its tail high. Turning briefly to glance at me, it disappeared behind the partially open gate. It seemed to be inviting me in.

I walked to the gate and followed the cat beyond the wall. The high black tail waved gently between banks of flowers on either side of a brick path before me. I looked around to see the most beautiful garden. Borders full of flowers, shrubs and vegetables, were symmetrically divided by paths. Plants spilled over in abundance and ahead the cat was weaving slightly between the stems and flowers falling onto the path. This wasn't a garden that had gone to seed. Someone was looking after it and growing vegetables, and fruit. My eye was drawn to trees at the back of the borders, espaliered against the warm red walls. One of them looked like apricots. I didn't know which way to turn, there was so much to see, and who had done it all? The cat was still walking steadily towards the centre of the garden, and I felt compelled to follow. The air was warm and heavy with scent in this secret garden. There was a background humming of insects and faint birdsong but all felt quiet and drowsy. Ahead of me, the cat had stopped in the centre of the garden and was sitting upright, regarding me again. There was a circular bench around a huge pot with a tree in it, and I had a ridiculous feeling that the cat expected me to sit down. This was such a mystery. As I lowered myself on to the bench, a low distant rumble echoed across the sky. I hesitated. Thunder? There had been no mention of that on the weather forecast this morning. I sat down and the cat jumped up and sat next to me. "Well Puss?" I looked down, "this is a lovely garden you've got here." The cat seemed to be surveying the garden ahead of it. "Who looks after it? And you?" The cat didn't even acknowledge that I had spoken. I was beginning to feel as if I'd strayed into the past, a lost world.

An incredibly loud clap of thunder, right overhead, made me jump. I, or the thunder, must have startled the cat too as it leapt up, poised on the edge of the bench. A pang of disappointment passed through me but, before I could do anything, the heavens opened and a heavy curtain of rain swept down. The cat dashed off the bench and away along the path. I rushed after it, trying to dodge the drooping wet vegetation. The cat's tail was down now and its ears back as it ran. I lurched along behind it, gasping at the coldness of the sudden drenching. Instantly, my clothes were sodden and my hair in rat's tails across my face. Big drips ran into my eyes and made me blink. The cat veered to the left and through a door that magically appeared ahead. I stumbled after it into a glasshouse, thankful to get out of the downpour. The cat had stopped and was looking at me. No longer regal and proud but dishevelled, its fur spikey with the rain. A puddle was forming around my feet and trickles worked their way down my scalp and body. I crouched and stretched my hand out to the cat. "Thanks, Puss, I'm glad to get out of that." The cat moved forward, sniffed my hand, and rubbed its cheek against my fingers.

Welcome to the Garden by Katherine Miskin

Ah, hello, hello there, come along, come on in.

Yes, very good, welcome. Welcome to our little garden. I say "our", of course, my better half is in charge, really. I just do the bits I can be trusted with, you know.

Anyway, yes, come on through, are you ok there on that path? I know, it's a bit lethal with the wild thyme growing up through the cracks like that. And do mind those thorns on the roses on the wall as you come through the walkway. Oh dear, has it snagged your jacket? I am most sorry, I really am.

So here we are, my favourite bit of the whole place. You can go and look at the borders and the other bits later, but I'd really like to show you around the kitchen garden first. I really am very proud of this bit, and I'm allowed to do all the weeding here since everything's in straight lines and even I can't mess it up here.

So, first off, just look at these fruit trees. The walls here were one of the reasons we bought the place, you know, we both felt that it would be so ideal for training fruit trees. So, we've got apples and plums and that's even a nectarine there in the corner although it hasn't done so much yet. You'll have to come again in a few months, the apple harvest is looking like it'll be first class.

Then the soft fruit there, can't beat raspberries and blackcurrants straight off the bushes, can you? Yes, go on, do help yourselves, we can never get through it all to be honest.

And then, this really is my favourite bit, this little bit paved with bricks in the corner, where the bench is in front of the potting shed. I can sit here quite happily for hours. It's the perfect spot to sit, of course, if you're shelling peas or top-and-tailing the gooseberries. And I'm really very pleased that we had enough bricks to do the whole of the path through the vegetable garden – it divides up the sections so nicely.

Ah, now I've been very disappointed with the beans this year. We just can't get them started off before the slugs get them, every time. They've been sown three times now. That's why they're so small still. Oh, do you really think they'll catch up? Let's hope.

No, they're sprouts, I know, they do look curious don't they? Oh, don't you? I like them, myself.

And here we are now, at the cut through in the hedge through to the rest of the garden. I'll let you explore that bit yourselves, I'm not so good at all the names of the flowers and things. I'll just sit here and if you need anything just give us a shout.

Oh heavens, quick, come back through here, yes, mind you don't slip over. I know, I've never seen rain like it. Well, of course, one says that doesn't one? But you know what I mean!

Yes, yes, come through into the greenhouse here. We can wait it out.

Goodness, isn't it loud on the roof in here? Sorry? Yes, that's what I said!

I say, look at it, those beans are battered down, we'll be too late now to sow them yet again, what a shame. I do enjoy runner beans.

Oh, and look at the way it's running down the brick paths. Yes, I agree, it does bring out the colours in the bricks rather nicely, doesn't it? They look very vibrant. And it's really rather nice you know, seeing the way the rain splashes up so high when it hits the ground. Although it'll make an awful mess with the way it's splashing the soil about onto the path.

So unexpected, wasn't it just? I check the forecast every morning as well. Who would have thought it could get so dark so very quickly?

Oh dear, and we'd just made a final sowing of carrots to squeeze another small crop in before the winter – those seeds are going to be swimming away now, aren't they? Look at this little brook we've got now running along the edge here. Oh, and what a large puddle – I had no idea the area around the greenhouse was so low compared with the rest of the garden.

Gosh, yes, those shoes really will get ruined, won't they? Well, I expect we can find some bricks or something as stepping stones.

Painting Masqueville Gardens by Katie Lloyd

At first light she had carried her easel, bag and umbrella through the overgrown ferns and tendrils of ivy. Around her reddening bramble slumped under the weight of the summer gone. She was surprised at how unkempt this part of the garden was. She wondered how many other areas, hidden from your usual visitor, were left to go back to nature in this way. The gardener, who seemed as old as the house and gardens, had protested vociferously against her heading up to this plateau. Which only made her more determined to paint from this very spot.

The view was tremendous. The gold of the acers and red of the scarlet oaks created an explosion of fireworks against the green of the surrounding gardens and the countryside beyond. The air was still, almost expectant, with a pale blue sky that concealed a sharp chill. She set to work.

As the sun traced across the sky, finer details of the different gardens were highlighted. Light and shade move sinuously, shifting from colour to colour. Features which were invisible in the morning, like the pool in the Rhododendron Garden and the ring of statues in the Italian Garden, were coming to life in the gentle afternoon light. Hidden secrets of the landscape were revealed and then lost once again as the sunlight moved on. She worked steadily, trying to capture the transforming gardens around her. All the time she was aware that the gardener was lingering, watching her under the pretence of nearby work. She pulled her scarf tighter and glanced wearily at the approaching bank of yellow cloud.

Her large umbrella had kept the lowing sunlight at bay but now she watched as it sheltered her from the fine snowflakes that were starting to silently drift to the ground around her. Teasingly they twisted and tumbled, gaining in speed and density. They landed, flake upon flake, smothering colour and light, definition and detail. In minutes the landscape had been robbed of its identity: the gardens cloaked of their secrets and transformed to a blank canvas.

Out of the corner of her eye she saw the gardener stand, admiring the scene with his hands on his hips, before picking up his tools and trudging back through the snow towards the house. She sighed and put down her paint brush. She had no option but to do the same.

The Tour of Tregurnock by Julian Crooks

(Part One)[8]

It was obvious that he was not enjoying himself. Hands in pockets, for the most part eyes downcast looking at his feet. It felt like he was barely listening to a word she was saying. Even if he didn't tell her so directly, Jim's body language told Helen all she needed to know: 'How much more of this is there? Can we go back now?'

'And this is the most special place of the whole garden,' she continued. Her sweeping gesture took in the new vista that had suddenly opened up before them. A seemingly hidden ravine, lush and vibrant, dotted with exotic and sub-tropical plants. From their position perched at the head of this unexpected valley they gazed down on mature fronds of thick-trunked tree ferns and the spikey fan-tops of chusan palms perhaps fifteen metres high. How so completely different from the stately lawns and formal borders, typical of many nineteenth century houses, that they had just encountered here at Tregurnock. In this part of the garden (hardly a garden!) there were no neatly trimmed evergreen hedges, concealing here and there an alcove into which was set a neo-classical plinthed statue of a Greek or Roman goddess or nymph. The blaze of summer colour of the herbaceous borders, deep with rich swathes of rudbeckia, echinacea and leucanthemum, a

---

[8] The following work was completed as a three-part task.

playground for frolicking painted ladies and red admirals was replaced by sombre shades of earthy greens with here and there a bright, slightly surreal spike of gaudy mauve or vivid lemon. The welcome breeze they had felt just ten minutes previously, that had swept towards them from the fields in the distance and over the unseen ha-ha to alleviate the burning heat of the sun was no more. Now the air was humid and heavy, decidedly still and tropical. The faint trickling and bubbling that rose to their ears through the glossy fronds of the canopy indicated the promise of a hidden stream possibly leading to sultry and sheltered pools plentiful in insect and birdlife.

If he wasn't exactly impressed he did at least show some interest, his raised eyebrows betraying a natural surprise. Encouraged, Helen pressed on ahead down the roughly cut steps which descended diagonally towards the centre of the ravine. She explained the garden's story: how a new owner of the estate had, in the 1920s, discovered the ravine almost by accident and, assuming it to be just another piece of wild and overgrown south Cornish woodland had left it alone and untouched for a full ten years. It was only when one of the elderly ex-nurses had come to visit (the house had operated as a sanatorium for injured and shell-shocked soldiers during the Great War) that an unsuspected secret came out. A previous owner of the estate had, in the last twenty years of his life, either side of the turn of the century, undertaken several arduous expeditions to the Himalayas and even the high Andes in search of exotic and unusual plants that might thrive in the sub-tropical Cornish micro-climate that this natural ravine offered. And thrive they did and the ravine was miraculously transformed into a private Eden that justified the efforts and satisfied the passion of the old man.

Sadly, the estate had suffered though, as had many others the length and breadth of the nation, from the departure of estate workers, including all but one of the gardeners, for the trenches of northern France and Flanders. The formal gardens around the main house were left barely tended and the ravine itself, a glorious and lush sub-tropical paradise, isolated at the far end of the estate was necessarily spurned. Left to its own devices this botanical paradise, unchecked, inevitably transformed itself into thick, choking jungle. 'And even though they restored the formal gardens quickly, this ravine took much longer,' Helen continued, 'it's still pretty wild in places.'

'Not for humans!' exclaimed Jim, catching hold of a branch that whipped back at him as Helen pushed swiftly on. 'Wait till you see the Captain's Pools!' said Helen over her shoulder. 'It's absolutely magical! They say when it's really quiet you sometimes hear... Hello! What's this?' As she had turned down a side track almost hidden from the main path they found their way was prematurely barred by an old wheelbarrow – it seemed to have been placed across the path, permitting no further progress, clearly suggesting their way should be the main path, not this less obvious path. 'Must be one of the gardeners, wonder why it's here though?' Helen deftly moved the barrow to one side and Jim followed her into a denser, darker patch of undergrowth that soon began to fringe into the path itself and over their heads slowing their pace. The sounds of birds that had echoed through the ravine became muted and then disappeared as the thick vegetation crowded around them. It was as though they had entered a subterranean tunnel, airless, dank and hot. What they saw next stopped them dead in their tracks.

What Happened Next at Tregurnock by Julian Crooks

(Part Two)

The old man looked as shocked by their presence as they were by his. For a moment all three held their breath, the heavy air seemed to vibrate with the tension. 'This ain't the right path for yous!' A harsh accent, an accusing stare. 'Only the gardener down 'ere!' Helen, flustered, mumbled an apology for their trespass, supremely conscious of her embarrassment which was two-fold: at having ignored the gardener's crude but clear sign that the wheelbarrow indicated no access to this private space, but also at her sense of humiliation in front of Jim.

At the loud crack of thunder Helen and Jim instinctively glanced up. It was close by and the deep shuddering rumble hidden within the unseen clouds continued for some time betokening a storm of unusual excess. The gardener, who seemed to take no notice of either the crack or the ensuing rumble, had already turned, shouting at them to follow him quickly to the shelter. They hurried after his retreating figure and within just a few steps the tunnel of vegetation had opened out. Now the canopy, clinging to both sides of the ravine, was gratifyingly visible again. It seemed to be holding the glowering, heavy-clouded sky at bay. Some distance ahead, close to the edge of a pool fringed with tall reeds and huge, prehistoric umbrellas of gunnera, they could just about make out a small, rustic shed.

The first leaden drops spattered through the branches and plashed all around. The old man sped on swiftly with a sureness of foot remarkable for his years. The second crack of thunder exploded above them: a deafening boom. Equatorial rain bulleted down like a grey, iron curtain. Scooping her lank hair out of her eyes, feeling her thin dress plastered to her skin, Helen ran as fast as she dare. The roar of the deluge echoing from all sides, a world suddenly stripped of colour. A pulse beat in her temples. One foot slipped in the mud and she shrieked like a child as she lost her balance, regained it and rushed on, Jim's heavy footsteps splashing behind her, his panting drowned out by the din of rain and rumble of thunder.

The ancient wooden shelter, open on the side facing the pool, welcomed them in. Hands on knees, bent double, the pair of them struggled to regain their breath. 'Like I said,' gasped Jim, 'not for humans!' It was only when they looked up and met each other's eyes that they realised they were alone in the shelter: the old gardener was not with them.

The Gardener's Secret by Julian Crooks

(Part Three)

There was a crude wooden bench fixed to the back of the open shelter. They sat down exhausted. From here they could look out over almost the entire pond, from the gushing feadan on their right, now a rushing torrent, to the small island complete with its specimen acer palmatum directly in front of them, to the deeply rush-fringed margin to their left. Even as they watched, regaining their breath and composure after the exertions of their run for cover, the rain abated. Calm settled on the pond. As quickly as they had appeared the slate-grey storm clouds gave way to bursts of bright sunshine which glared and shone from the wet vegetation. On cue the garden responded: birdsong rang out and echoed around the little valley, the sub-tropical fronds and leaves seemed to push up and splay themselves in homage to the sun. For a moment Helen closed her eyes and sensed the soothing intensity of the natural world.

She opened her eyes and immediately a sharp movement draw her attention to the corner of the shelter. 'What on earth is that?' She beckoned Jim and they approached the heap of gardening implements left haphazardly in the corner. An old and rather grimy board fashioned out of cork had been placed upon the wall. Pinned in neat rows upon the board were a series of butterflies – or to be more precise the wings of butterflies missing the body of the insect itself. 'What an odd place for a collection,' she whispered, 'and what an odd collection.' Most of the butterflies were recognisable but some were not – they were clearly foreign, presumably tropical, species in a quite dazzling array of colours and patterns. One in particular held her attention. Not a typical butterfly shape, but with much wider and narrower wings that would fit a short-bodied insect. The wings were fabulously iridescent – a deep, glossy emerald, edged with spots of the purest white. She could imagine how with slow, languorous flaps the butterfly would shimmer as it rose and fell and rose again on the slightest breath of wind. Its beauty quite took her breath away.

'Please help, lady!' piped a thin voice. So soft and high pitched was the call that both Helen and Jim believed they had imagined it. The call was repeated like the 'tseep' of a baby robin begging its parents for food. 'Down here!' Helen's eyes opened wide as for once in her life she was speechless.

The spider's web had been spun across the opening of the watering can. An old, galvanised and rather dirty watering can. The gardener, for it was he, was stuck fast, glued to the grasping gossamer strands at the very centre of the web. He was helpless, arms spread wide with a terrified and rather pathetic expression on his sunburnt face. Helen was immediately reminded of the gory crucifix positioned ominously by the lych-gate to greet visitors to St Saviour's. Whilst Helen had puzzled since her early childhood as to why the carved wooden effigy of Christ should display such a curiously submissive and benign expression in the face of certain death, she had no such doubt as to the reason for the assertion of terror that twisted the poor gardener's wrinkled features. The advancing spider tripping delicately along the stretched silken strands would make short shrift of him – a juicy meal indeed! Normally paralysed with fear at the sight of any creature with more than the regulation four legs, Helen found herself reaching quickly into her purse, locating the eyebrow tweezers and, with great dexterity, plucked the hungry arachnid from its home and flung it towards the pond.

She gently extricated the gardener from his gossamer gaol and placed him in her palm. He seemed quite calm – thankful, but trusting too. Once he had recovered his composure he began to explain, in his reedy falsetto, how he had fallen into the web after slipping out of one of the butterfly costumes. It could be argued, he told her somewhat philosophically, that the spider had done him a favour, since if his fall had not been broken by the web he would have plopped straight into the scummy, murky depths of the watering can – and he wasn't a good swimmer.

'Which pair of wings was it?' Helen asked.

'The grianon,' said the old man. 'They were a gift, quite new. I did so want to fly over the pond as soon as the rain had stopped – there's nothing better than floating through the rising pond-mist after a storm!' He indicated the grianon on the corkboard but his mouth fell open. The beautiful emerald iridescent wings were gone!

'Jim, what happened to the wings?' asked Helen, remembering her companion. But as she turned round she saw that Jim was gone too.

An introduction to: Landscape Writing Inspired by Photography

The following pieces of work were created using the technique of taking a landscape photograph and splitting it into three equal horizontal sections. The writers were then asked to choose one section of either photograph to describe in detail. For clarity the pieces have been organised into Top, Middle or Bottom to indicate which section of the image is being described. Once read back we discovered a rich description of both images using only words. The words were inspired by the two images on the following pages. Image A of a waterfall and Image B of an upland landscape.

Landscape Photography by Tim Oxburgh[9]

Image A, photograph by Tim Oxburgh:

[9] You can find Tim on Instagram @c_r_a_g_r_a_t

Image B, Photograph by Tim Oxburgh:

Image A Descriptions

The Waterfall by Sharon Linden

(Image A top)

High above a rocky gorge, chiselled away by time, the sun filters through the canopy of a myriad tiny leaves, anchored securely to slender, outstretched arms. From along one rugged crag fresh life springs, soaking up the warm, generative light. With roots tightly woven into each available crevice, they determinedly flourish and thrive.

    Not so fortunate, on the opposite face, the inhabitants of the shade. Their equal resoluteness has failed them, their coppery, dried remains swaying lifelessly in the steady summer breeze. A gentle mist ascends, hinting at what lies beneath, and overhead, the constant chorus of winged creatures competing hopelessly with the thunderous rumblings below.

A Fine Mist by Steven Mitchell

(Image A top)

A fine mist rises in the shady, narrow valley. Verdant moss pillows, dripping with moisture hug the steep, sharp rock. And in crevices, seeds have fallen, sprouting small trees whose roots desperately cling to the valley sides, sending their limbs high to seek escape and sunlight.

The air carries the aroma of damp flora, and from somewhere deep below rises the sound of rushing water.

The place feels untouched, like I'm the only person who's stumbled on this secret.

Waterfall by Hilary Park

(Image A middle)

Somewhere people are talking and perhaps there is news and I know there is haste and roads keep on roaring. Somewhere digital mouths constantly comment on not so much and there are all those other things that we have inflicted on ourselves. But here, there is the white sound of a river rushing clean to the edge of rock. It doesn't pause but, like sudden spilt milk, dashes random and cold to the floor of the earth below. There it catches the light, flowing golden over boulders of all shapes and sizes. It is music in motion, hypnotic in its journey from one place to another. Let me tell you how softly the air soaks up the river, the way the sweetness of sap seeps into the scent of weather until each misted breath I take leads me deeper into the atmosphere of forest. The soaked stone surrounds me exhaling the damp years, my senses swim as though I were the brown trout nosing the riverbed. Sometimes the high sharp call of a jay tears ragged across calm thoughts and leaps my heart from its place. Prehistoric shapes then loom above me as I lean small against the stern body of the ravine. Its rough surface, glass sharp against my skin, is sketched with lichen – bright fluorescent scribbles of lime and ink punctuated with firedots of yellow. Intricate weavings of fern, curtain down like springtime as though the stone, cool and bronze as it seems, has become tree – reaching through green for the far, pale sky. Plump roundels of moss coat the monolith beside me and it rests diagonal, as though it is lulled harmless by the rhythm of water. Inside my head I can almost hear its crashing fall, almost feel the force of air against its weight, like the ancient tombstone of an angry god, it toppled, but when I do not know. Now it sleeps and waits for stories to be told, for someone to inscribe it with fine words. High above, a breeze catches on birch and leaves seem to flicker, some floating down like coins into a fountain. The waterfall absorbs the forest's offerings, moving life on, swirling it forward, feeding its river through the seasons sometimes fiercely, sometimes with a silver caress. Somewhere people are talking and perhaps there *is* news but here the voice of the river is fresh and true and clean.

Glinting by Sarah Carlin

(Image A bottom)

Glinting

A snoozing dinosaur in the foreground?

With water behind it, dancing like a nymph away down the rocks.

An earthly muted rainbow from celadon,

To cerulean, back to brown, then rust and dragon's blood.

The light sparkles on the slippery rocks and moss.

On their uneven and cleaven shapes,

Glinting like diamonds or emeralds.

Is it a woosh and swoosh, or a trickle and tickle?

A gush and a flush, as the foam collects below.

Grey Boulders and Waterfalls by Rebecca Banks

(Image A bottom)

The water remembers the route through the rocks. It hurries on, soothing scarred red stone, liberating the littlest of fragments to join it on its journey. A jumbled congregation of marbled and mossed onlookers watch the water, and they wonder at the urgent energy of the water travelling onwards. They sit peacefully, like reclining grey seals after a welcome feast. The endless music of the stream fills the still air.

Image B Descriptions

The God of Anger by Nicky Hutchison

(Image B top)

The God of Anger has drained the mountains to monochrome. On the far skyline they are white, chill and impassive, trapped as they are in his cold rage. Now he is coming for the scarred, brown-heathered hills either side of the valley, to leach away the light and hope of their soft slopes. They steadfastly hold their ground as their far edges blacken with his wrath. Spots of sunlight catch the near flanks trying to lighten the mood before the last stand. A rocky outcrop has already run for the hills and sits atop watching the drama unfold, his strategy as yet unknown.

The sky's iron eyebrows scowl darkly over the gentle glen. A white furrow creases the grim forehead, lightning ready to rip and scar the valley sides. Pressure builds and rumbles like the start of a bitter fight that will clear the air.

Wild by Katie Lloyd

(Image B top)

Bruised and threatening, the sky hangs heavy over mountaintops. Brighter chinks of smothered sunshine reflect the snow which webs the highest peaks. This white against the dark rippled ridge reminds me of the foaming crests of waves, building and rising for the inevitable fold and fall into a crash of sea spray and rock.

A bitter and relentless wind adds to the anticipation of more snow to come. It carries the cronk of a raven, an unseen detail in the entanglement of light and dark.

In the mountainside inky crags and crumples hold shadowed secrets of wildlife – an old peregrine nest, a ptarmigan feather, a resilient and determined pine sapling.

As a golden eagle, if I were to glide through the monochrome wilderness, I would pick out a lofty perch on which to pluck my prey and observe my territory. My golden nape illuminating the scene.

The Green Valley by Sharon Williamson

(Image B middle)

The green valley lies hidden among ochre hillsides that rise away steeply. A glacier surely ground the valley bottom flat, in another age altogether. The gentle pocket of green is divided up by dry stone walls, like a board game in the landscape; here and there trees follow the lines, even up the valley sides and beyond. A haven from the harsh hills and fells, the valley is a gleaming green jewel hidden in a fold amid the rolling high ground of rough grasses, stony cliffs and boulders.

Looking out at the View by Charlotte Dale

(Image B middle)

Looking out at the view of this landscape is like viewing a bowl of colour. The pleasant green patchwork of fields sit at the centre of surrounding hills and mountains. The fields are dotted with trees that form the valley floor. Whilst elevated all around are not granite peaks, but bracken covered ridges at varying heights. Browns, golds and yellows tinged with pink make up the pallet of these mountains. The scene appears distant and we're unable to view the backdrop or mountain peaks. But the valley floor tells us the sun is somewhere, trying to escape the clouds and as we inhale the air is pure.

Manmade by Katie Lloyd

(Image B middle)

Fawn and rust-edged slopes slide steeply into the valley. Rivets made by water and ice line the hillsides, leading into a drained bowl of fertile green fields.

   Up here, bristles of brown-ochre rushes mark linear flushes and down there, in winter, black hackles of trees and barely-there hedgerows compartmentalise the greener-looking grass.

   Zipped up to the chin and tucked into hat and hood, if I were to reach that stone wall, with its round and mossy, perfectly placed stones, I would crouch for shelter from the unforgiving wind. Consider where my boots end and the earth begins.

The Valley Floor by Patricia Martin

(Image B middle)

The steep sided hills give way to a broad green valley floor, the richness of the smooth green fields, divided by stone walls, and some hedgerow, contrasting with the rough brown scrub and grey scree of the surrounding hillsides. A stream wends its way from the far funnel of the hills and scattered houses and farmsteads can be seen, remote but wealthy with rich pasture.

There is a lonely cottage on the edge of the valley where the land slopes more gently upwards, a land of rough pasture, grazed by a single cow, a belted Galloway perhaps, maybe the house cow for the isolated steading.

Above, the hills rise up towards a range of mountains, snow layered, and the sky heavily grey with rain, but where the storm clouds part, sunlight plays across the steep brown hillside, changing the rough unforgiving surface momentarily into patches of pure, soft gold.

From the cottage, the ground slopes towards us in a gentler fashion; the rough pasture has been grazed this summer around scattered outcrops of lichen covered rock, akin to the 'grey wethers' found in other parts of the country but maybe these rocks are of a harder stone, resilient like the distant mountains and the valiant hills.

Landscape by Elizabeth Fairweather

(Image B middle)

I'm just having a breather here and a drink. The dry, yellowy grass I'm sitting on is prickly, unlike the fields further along the valley floor.

Those undulating pockets of rich green are split by ribbons of pale pathways and short rows of trees.

Rising solemnly behind the fields are the sombre, magnificent grey mountains. My eyes can follow them up to the sky. Tiny spots of green daub the mountainsides. It's amazing what can cling to life in such inhospitable conditions.

The air is warm on my face as I soak up the view. No-one else seems to have ventured this way.

But I am not alone here in this wild place. I can hear buzzards mewing and looking up, see a pair soaring on the thermals, high above me. I wonder if they can see me?

How wild and free this place is. How intoxicating in its vastness. There doesn't seem to be much cover here for anything, though I think I can make out the odd little bird perching on the stick-like hedges close by. There must be some little creatures and insects if I watch and wait for long enough.

But it looks like a storm is brewing in the blackening sky, so I must press on.

Standing above the Treeline by Jenny Cooper

(Image B middle)

I'm standing above the tree line on a hill looking down into the apex of a horseshoe valley. Towering hills either side remind me of the Scottish Highlands. Numerous grass fields carpet the valley floor, divided by low stone walls, although no livestock can be seen. Along some of the walls are conifers. At the bottom of the hill where I am standing are a couple of dwellings, one either side of the valley.

The Shadows are Coming! by Berenice Tregenna

(Image B bottom)

The hard, grey rocks are speckled about like splinters on the ground. The short, yellowing grass under my feet is like a worn carpet where many people have been. I stand and pause for a moment on a soft patch, listening to distant thunder and feeling apprehension. I'm hoping the ominous clouds in the distance, casting deep shadows across the mountain tops, don't come this way. I am unable to hear birdsong, probably because of the inclement weather and lack of trees nearby. There is a sense of foreboding in this tired land. I feel the cold to my bones, I must walk on but careful not to trip on those shards beneath me...

These Lumps of Stone by Julian Crooks

(Image B bottom)

Who dropped these lumps of stone? They may be modest chunks of ancient granite decorated with lichens, but they are much too heavy for you or I to lug, panting and sweating – it must have been a passing giant, journeying down from the distant mountain tops. Here they lie, solid, permanent on the close-cut turf, once a startling vivid green, now pale and jaundiced through lack of rain on this late summer afternoon. The slab closest to us is a thin wedge of grey, granite cheese – a small table-top perfect for thrushes to smash the shells of snails. Except there are no thrushes here; this upland is open and devoid of trees. This is the home of the curlew, its bubbling call flowing magically over this lonely place following closely its gently fluctuating contours. These other low rocks scattered around us are lookout and songposts for the nondescript meadow pipit (the poor man's skylark) or its sartorial opposite the wheatear flamboyantly twerking its handsome but subtle fuselage of buff and pearl-grey.

   Under these lowering skies the light is diffused and the mood sombre. The chill wind bites our cheeks and nips our fingers as it races up from the valley to share its mountain top scents. The occasional chink in the oppressive, melancholy clouds surprisingly brings not a hint of joy or warmth but of menace. These gloomy granite shards around us are actually offcuts of the sky. Ah, that's how they came to be here…

Tamed by Katie Lloyd

(Image B bottom)

Short, moss-filled turf blankets the ground like gold-flecked crushed velvet. It is pockmarked by rocks mapped with lime green lichen. The silence of absent grasshoppers and crickets, echoes the missing skylarks and meadow pipits. The damp wood-earth scent of moss and peat lingers.

As a tree, if I were able to push roots down through the soil and anchor stubbornly, I would wait for the chance to grow beyond the moss and the regular bite of deer and sheep. And when that time comes, I will reclaim the landscape for myself.

Introduction: Creating Images through Art

The following pieces of work were created by writers choosing a piece of work from an artist introduced during the writing task, or a favourite artist of their own.

Art can be a different and exciting way to connect with the natural world, and helps us to explore our internal feelings through the way that artists have represented landscape or their relationship with nature through visual imagery. By exploring realistic painting in detail and imagining being stood alongside the artist as they created the piece we can bring the landscape to life in our imagination. The movements of a brush stroke can indicate the energy of the landscape and the feeling of natural elements. Colour can illuminate a scene, recreating the warmth of the sun, or the heavy feeling before a storm.

Abstract art inspired by the natural world can help us to understand emotions and relationships with nature on a deeper level. When you look at a painting and try to describe it through words, we can tap into the inner world of the artist bringing the imagery to the surface of our writing. Sometimes a colour, or pattern can remind us of something significant in our own lives and help us to reconnect with nature by bringing a feeling back into focus.

Keeping a nature journal that includes drawing and writing can help us to deepen our own connections.

Almond Blossom by Katie Lloyd

(Inspired by Almond Blossom by Vincent Van gough,1890)

The sweet-scented air and the thrum of the first bees of the year distract me from the throb in my toes and fingers. I pull my shawl tighter as the early spring chill seeps down my neck and Vincent stops to blow hot air into his cupped hands. As the sun rises higher, the bees get more plentiful and the white blossom radiates against the clear sky, reflecting the melting snow beneath our feet.

The Walker by Sharon Williamson

Early one winter morning, the walker and his dog left the village and followed their usual footpath, along the drain through fields of dark, peaty earth. The flat lands lay under a vast sky; you could watch the weather arriving from miles away. This morning was cold and damp; a haze of mist was still clinging low in patches, but the sky was clear. The freshness of the early start and the stillness of the air meant that scents hung deliciously, and the dog was busy sniffing out all the delights – the fox that had passed by, the rabbits in the banks of the drain, the hares alert in the fields.

The walker was not privy to this particular sensory world. He saw the winter geese and swans flying in to feed in the fields, and he gazed out at the endless monochrome lands, the straight drains and dykes, but his mind was turned inwards and his focus was entirely somewhere else.

Summer Fields by Katherine Miskin

Inspired by Kurt Jackson's work, "Summer Fields"

Early one morning he lay, half way to wakefulness, in the long cool grass at the bottom of the hedge. The tickle of a tiny spider running across his arm made him shift and wake.

The patchwork of fields stretched out below the hillside, mile upon mile of scorched brown stubble and parched yellow hay fields. Even at this early hour, the sun was hot and the air smelt of dusty earth and hot grass. The sky was a deep clear blue, with a band of indigo sea between sky and land. He longed for a drink.

Far up in the sky, a buzzard soared, a plaintive mewing in the air.

He sat up, head swimming. Skylarks rose from the fields beneath him, tripping themselves up with their desperate trilling songs. A bee lazily buzzed past his head, investigating the flowers along the hedge line. The sudden scolding of a blackbird, shooting out from the hedge, made him start. Unsteadily, he got to his feet and surveyed the land before him.

He had to get to the sea.

Inspired by a painting by Aelbert Cuyp

Herdsman with Five Cows by a River 1650 to 1655 - by Charlotte Dale

Early one morning the billowing clouds reflected in the lake as the fishermen counted their catch. The two men dressed for warmth wearing felt hats sat hunched in their small wooden rowing boat. Silver scales glistened on their fingers in the dawn light. Their day was nearly over but the herdsman's had just begun.

The herdsman spoke softly to his cattle as they calmly grazed at the river's edge. Each day was long and hard but as a nearby skylark sang its descending song the herdsman knew he couldn't possibly leave for the city. Sailing boats bobbed in the distance as overhead the vibrating wings of a skein of geese were yet to arrive at their day's grazing ground. How easy it would be to arrive each morning at a new destination, feed and then leave as dusk falls. But like the mining bees excavating in the soft sandstone cliffs behind, his time and energy was invested here – for life.

Saint-Rémy-de-Provence, July 1889 by Hilary Park

Inspired by Vincent van Gogh (1853 – 1890)

Air in this dark corner of the garden has soaked up the conversation of the copse and become part of the complexity. Inhaling is like diving down into a sea of moist forest, the velvet breath of moss and ivy fills me with the sedative of morning. Light sleeps in deep emerald shadows, leaping pale now and then in pollen smudges of sun flicking through the canopy. Half a dozen trees lean towards each other companionably whilst glossy shields of ivy grow thick, creaking on and coating trunks, turning their shadowy bark blue. I long to lay my hand on the dark curve of that tree or lie on the eiderdown of forest floor listening to time slowing. The terracotta earth is far below. It waits beneath layers of loam and vitality which leafs between the trees in swathes of thriving undergrowth. When the deep growing sous-bois reaches the border it breaks out into bright Spring, a golden band of energy bordering the stillness. Between the verdant night thoughts and the light beams of hope I think about Vincent. His short brushstrokes of oily paint seething from the asylum transformed into new greens stretching the knowledge of my eye and texturing life with the magic of his imagination.

The Colour of My World by Julian Crooks

Inspired by The Sower (Arles 1888) by Vincent Van Gogh

Although the sun was sitting almost on the horizon it was no less comfortable to look at. By squinting towards the great flaming ball I had offered my cheeks and the sun, like a bully, had slapped them. Burning skin stretched taut across my face.

I looked carefully at the artist's easel. 'What's the secret?' I asked, 'where do these colours come from?' His canvas had astonished me. A welter of incandescence that shouted and screamed at the viewer. A blueless sky, a chrome-yellow disc confined within a band of shimmering lemon-yellow. Below, another horizontal band, this one of harvest-ready ochre corn; and then the largest band, a substantial rectangle of disguised earth – a sprightly dabbing of incongruent blues (from teal to cobalt), umber and burnt sienna that jarred yet fascinated.

No less astonishing the agility, deftness and sheer confidence as, utterly absorbed, his hand moved swiftly, methodically over the canvas. It was clear I was not part of his world. How could I be, he was creating a new world in front of my very eyes. What was his secret? From where did his gift come?

He turned momentarily as I repeated my question. His piercing blue gaze held mine fiercely, but his words were as gentle as the earth. 'Close your eyes. Feel what's around you, what you're a part of – then you can paint. Only then can you try to paint.'

I did as he bid me. Eyelids not quite closed the sun burst between the lashes igniting streaks of golden flame. The slightest of breezes tickled the hairs on my arms. Faint cracks of crows drifted over from my left. And from the earth beneath me, all around me, rose the rich odour of the humble field-blooms, of the dank, defeated Provençal soil, the serene hum of insects, the vibrations of the earth itself. And all of these challenged the dominance of the sun, became the shadows on the canvas. And now I understood the cluttered dabs approximating a darkness produced magically by discordant, jarring shades. Without this shade you cannot truly glory in the sunlight.

He looked at me once more. 'We may worship the sun,' he said, 'but we should never forget the earth.'

Bittersweet Vincent and Paul by Sarah Carlin

I look across at the man painting next to me. Sulkily, and unobserved from under the wide brim of my hat. The smell of the sweet hay in the air, the mustiness of the ground beneath my feet. A sharp intake of breath or is it a sigh? He is painting flat, angular shapes, muted colours. I appraise my own canvas. Mine is a riot of colour and smudges of paint in all directions.

"What do you see?" I ask him. "The light…" he says. "The light it's like nothing I've ever seen before, the sky, it is like a rainbow, a merging of colours, it is so difficult to comprehend, and even more difficult to capture."

He looks at his picture, and I watch as his eyes appraise it. His expression always seems to exude a sense of carefree confidence. "What do *you* see? He asks me with a wry smile. I pause, and look, try to really look at what is before me. In the glare and shimmer of the heat, my brain struggles to keep up with the information being provided, I shake my head and wipe my brow.

"Those hay bales, each blade of hay, no one is alike. They stick out at different angles everywhere, each one a different shade of gold." But how is that possible? I think to myself. Paul returns to his methodical and precise way of painting.

The sun beats down on us, this Provençal heat, the dryness, the stillness of the air, contrasted with the industriousness of the farmers as they work against the beat of time. I hear the cicadas croaking their loud rhythm, the flies buzz lazily around my head. And focused on that hum and beat, my thoughts retreat in upon themselves again.

I watch as the farmer's daughter walks slowly past, lopsided, carrying a pail that is far too heavy for her. What is she thinking about? Does she wonder what we two men are up to, wasting time in the field, whilst there is real, endless, farm work to be done? Or does she wish she could stop and look, and possibly even pick up a brush herself? Then I notice Paul looking over at her too, casting a slightly leering eye.

I try to paint the clouds. Their forms weave above my head, forming and reforming into elusive shapes, it's like god is playing with my sense of reason. He creates and recreates, I will never be able to capture their omnificence. I hear the sound of scythes swashing in the distance. Paul slaps a mosquito that has taken hold on his neck. "Vincent!", he calls over to me.

When I invited Gauguin down to this magical place, I hoped that we could share ideas and move towards developing our work. But now I realise I am still alone, as I always have been. We've argued over how we should express form and colour, and our viewpoints are so wildly different there is no possibility of brotherhood. We are both waspish, lost in our own worlds, I am quick to lose my temper and he goes silent and broods. Like an old married couple, who stay together through a lack of any other options. Our union has been bittersweet.

A tiring day. The sun starts to set across the field, the golds are now tinged with pinks and scarlets – vermillion, lake red, and ochre. I smell a waft of lavender on the breeze and the heat of the day is still intense, but it feels more like a soft velvet cloak now, rather than an itchy linen shirt.

We pack up our paints and easels, clap off the dust and bits of grass from the day and walk slowly back to the town. "Vincent, you look so desperate. Come, let's go to the bar and have a drink and some food, it always cheers the spirits!" Paul says.

I wish I could brush off the worries of the world so easily, I wish I could forget the harshness of the world as easily as he does. But I am stuck in the feeling for the sadness of the human condition, and I think it will drive me into despair.

FOLKLORE, MYTHOLOGY AND FANTASY WRITING

Introduction: Folklore, Mythology and Fantasy Writing

Our ability to use imagination and to story our lives sets us apart from other living species. Our traditions and habits have roots in folklore and mythology, stories that have been passed down generations of people, from times when stories were shared orally rather than through the written word.

To explore folklore and mythology we started with naturally found objects that were linked to superstition and folklore. We looked at 'touchstone' objects that we could handle and investigate as a start point to inspiration. This included items such as four-leaf clovers, hagstones and heather. I also encouraged the writers to delve into mythology linked to creatures, particularly types of birds.

I asked the writers to consider their own familiar landscapes and to play with inventing their own stories to explain how different aspects of the landscape had been formed. Part of the research for these tasks involved re-visiting popular folktales and using them as a start point to build a story. To help the writers to do this I chose to look at the well-known legend behind the Giant's Causeway in Ireland, as it is a tale that many people are familiar with. I asked the writers to re-visit the story of the Finn McCool and Benandonner and to consider what happened next in the tale. The results were both surprising and inventive!

Finally we considered how folklore and mythology tie in with fantasy writing and how we can use aspects of traditional tales to inspire a fantasy landscape or a different time and place that is home to fantastical creatures.

Owls by Julian Crooks

Regarded throughout history and across cultures as special birds Owls are perhaps in a league of their own. The myths and folklore that has grown around them since the Greeks and Romans is contradictory; they are linked with witchcraft and forebode evil events yet were often seen as animals of great wisdom to be venerated. Owls make many appearances in English folklore including these: the screech of an owl flying past the window of a sick person forebodes imminent death. Raw owl eggs given to children were meant to provide protection against developing alcoholism in later life and owl broth was given to young children as a cure for whooping cough. But my favourite is this explanation originating from a twelfth century Kentish preacher of the reasons for the owl's nocturnal habits: the owl stole the rose which was a prized beauty in the garden –as a punishment the other birds allowed the owl to only fly and feed during the hours of darkness.

White Heather by Phoebe Devenney

It was a rough sort of day with the weather competing with the landscape to see which could be more rugged. The wind wailed, it tore at the land as it threw itself across the gorse and heather. The moors: my very own thick, uncomfortable, wiry jumper of woven turtled greens and deep plums. I loved the spikes and thorns that laced the land and scratched and grazed my knocking knees like the unwelcome, unwanted knitted armour so loving crafted by my Granny's wrinkled hands. Across that itchy land I stumbled. Hair bellowing any which way, face stinging from the pin pricks of rain and the air so fresh it burnt my tongue. Feeling like a Celtic queen as I grappled with roping roots and prickly carpets.

There are a few select moments in life in which we are humbled by the realisation that this raging world is not our own but a land we share with much more important folk. To think I nearly missed such a gem had it not been for a toothed stone biting into my right heel. I had taken a brief pause to relieve the cheeky chappy from my boot and that's when I saw it... a perfect patch of snow. So elegant, so dainty, so prevailing in all this roguish chaos. Blossoming by my muddy boot lay a small bunch of white heather. It felt in need of protection from this dangerous world.

Granny's warbling voice rang through the wind: "A patch of white heather marks the grave of fairy kin." Her words dwindled into the icy caw of a lonesome magpie. Somehow it felt too cruel to think of there being a little less magic in the world, but I had not expected to feel quite so wounded by the deprivation. Almost a guttural instinct, without a question or sense of shame, I curtsied to the mournful wreath to solute the sorrow as it flew on. I don't know what I was expecting as I looked into the little nightgown flowers, only I don't think it was to see a little petaled face staring back at me with a softness and sympathy unlike any I had seen before. She lay down a heather bell and as it rang on, she faded into the breeze.

I can't be sure, I can't be certain that is, but I have never had much of an imagination and Granny always told me to believe in fairies and Granny is always right.

The Fen Tiger by Sharon Williamson

If you follow the footpath westwards out of the Cambridgeshire town of St Ives along the river you will pass, eventually, a secluded meadow, where high hedgerows and summer wildflowers abound. The river here has meandered away a little; slow and wide, it has left a rich and ancient legacy, green and lush. Look more closely and you may detect strange undulations, as if an outgoing tide has left ridges and rivulets in sand. A huge and ancient white willow stands, split and fissured, at the head of the meadow.

Here treads the fen tiger. The few who have seen her tell of a huge yellow cat with bright eyes and lithe body. As she wakes, she flexes her claws, and gouges great clefts into the willow to sharpen them. Stretching out, in her feline fashion, the fen tiger rakes her immense nails through the rich surface of the meadow, leaving behind ridges and furrows as witness to her silent ritual. She stalks in darkness, always hungry for her next meal, and melts away with the dawn, elusive as disappearing tendrils of mist.

Myths and Folklore by Charlotte Dale

A hag stone – I've always wondered what they were. When beachcombing or foraging in the natural world. There have been occasions when I've found a beautiful smooth stone with a hole. Drawn to it, I've always picked it up and kept it but I never knew their name or significance. But it is the clover that evokes a memory from when I was about 11 or 12. I was walking with my mum and dogs, across fields of clover. I remember wanting to find a four-leaf clover and knew then it was magical and lucky. I remember wanting this and looking down – and there was a four-leaf clover! I picked it and pressed it, keeping it for some time. I recall the leaves being quite large and an envious friend telling me I'd stuck a leaf on to make four! The cheek!

Just this year, my niece, who is not much younger than I was then, was across the fields with her dog and parents, who were saying, "you never find a four-leaf clover." My niece looked down and said, "what like this?" So maybe finding four-leaf clovers is just meant for little girls that believe in luck and magic?

An Elemental Bird by Sharon Williamson

In a snaw-grimet under the eaves of my house there nests a pair of swifts. Each year they return, arriving from the south to bring up a new brood. Their screaming cries slice the air, and in the early evening I watch as they tumble through the sky with their kin. One bird, however, always flies alone, away from the mawn and brec.

As she slidders and snipes, I see her transform: her dark sickle shape becomes a hole in the sky, then a steel-edged maol, then a wisp of fire, then a water spout, twisting through the atmosphere. I've heard tales of the phoenix, a bird of flame born from ashes; here, above me, is a bird of all the elements, air, earth, fire and water. Never alighting, always aloft, she is a creature of another world, and I wonder what other magic she can do.

Foxgloves by Charlotte Dale

I love the mythology, magic and folklore that is associated with so much in the natural world; trees, plants and animals. In particular – flowers. Common names of flowers often tell us about our social history and medicinal properties. My interest in flower folklore has grown in recent years and I'm always looking up flowers and what they represent. Out now is a brilliant bee friendly flower – the foxglove *Digitalis purpurea.*

I love the tale of Foxgloves getting their name. Once known as 'Folk's gloves,' meaning gloves that belong to the 'good folk,' – the fairies. It is said they lived in woodlands where the foxgloves grew and to pick foxgloves would cause offence to the fairies. Legend has it, a bad fairy gave these flowers to a fox, so the fox could wear them on his toes to quieten his footsteps when skulking through chicken roosts. It is also said the speckles inside the trumpet of the foxglove flower are the fingerprints of elves and fairies. There is much written about the foxglove, especially its medicinal properties for heart problems (that I understand are still used today). And apparently, foxgloves should never go on a ship and if you hear them ring, death is imminent!

Reference – *An Encyclopaedia of Plants in Myth, Legend, Magic and Lore* by Stuart Phillips

Breakfast with a Snaw-Grimet by Phoebe Devenney

A further grumble and grunt stifled the air as he kicked his way through the sodden leaves that lined that woodland floor. A few had plastered themselves to his thick, leathery feet to give him a rather fetching patch-work pair of socks. These sloppy golds and browns of tired oak leaves are perhaps the only essence of elegance this huffing little mound has ever embodied.

I pressed my cheek closer to the trunk of the mighty oak that I was crouched behind until its damp, mossy bark sank into my cheeks. I want to get closer but I hardly dare blink in case he should scarper should he realise that he was being watched and then, be gone forever.

    Perhaps he was the consequence of having cheese for lunch, or the lack of sleep courtesy of the storm from the night before, but how could my little head think of something so perfectly imperfect? After all, I could hear his gravelled snuffles and snorts as he shuffled about, I could smell the faint but pungent musk of lemons, no, orange? Ah no, it had to be... Pear Drops! Surely not all your senses could be deceived at once?

    It was these rummagings that had first drawn him to my attention. The splatters and plops of sloppy leaves invited the expectation to see a hungry blackbird searching for lunch, however, when I approached the cacophony, it soon became clear that these utterances could not be from a golden beak. It had to be a Snaw-

Grimet! A rumbling, grumbling, hairy mole-hill of a man which are only found in the most ancient of woods.

As I peeped from behind the trunk, I could see a whirlwind of leaves and twigs being blown into the air in heavy huffs and puffs of little care. As I studied the movement, I could see that there was a squat little barrel shape, all elbows and toes, blundering its little way about the trees. The first thing I noticed about him was his enormous feet; wider than he was tall with stubby toes like the caps of button mushrooms and no less dirty. So sweet and perfectly round, I just want to squeeze them! Huge ears poke out from under a floppy, dusty hat. His speckled skin hangs in saggy folds, draping his round little face like the curtains at a grand theatre – I wonder what drama they have framed.

He seems to have no legs which would perhaps explain his awkward shuffling movement which is most like the heaving of a great sack of potatoes over a whimpering shoulder. Instead, his palmates seem to bolt straight into his stained flannel shirt which, thankfully, blows loosely about his knobbly little self.

He can't be any taller than my ankle, but he seems almost too big for these woods.

His thick, wrinkled hands are clenched into tight, little fists that swing across his chest like dried prunes. Elbows out, on he marches in systematic circles. His head is down and he appears to be in search of something. He is so unashamedly rough and rugged, so unapologetically chaotic and yet, so charming, so in need to be held, like a toddler unlucky enough to suck on a lemon.

Then, suddenly, all halts as he leaps upon his treasure – a magpie feather. The rim of his hat bounces up, revealing his current eyes that twinkle like the glass heads of pins. Wiry whiskers stick out from random points across his face, but far from prickly, he seems more shrivelled than sharp.

Grasping with stumpy fingers, he clutches his prize before effortless flinging his matted beard over his left shoulder. Tangles in this grey, gorse web are the fingerprints of the mystical land with twigs and thorns woven amongst his thin hairs.

Under his beard, he had hidden a leather pouch that looked fit to burst. Out of its ruffled rim rocketed: more feathers, fungi and flowers. He stuffs the latest ingredient into his treasure-trove, whipped down his beard and off he blundered into the hollow of a neighbouring tree – his dark, damp, broody home.

He must be cooking something scrumptious, something most sublime. The most tantalisingly pleasing breakfast you could ever dream of... The Snaw- Grimet speciality... Maol. Maol is a thick, porridge-like broth with all the warmth of the woods stewed into each spoonful. I shall have to rush back home to try and work out his recipe.

Waking from Under the Hawthorn by Charlotte Dale

As I inhaled before opening my eyes, I was aware of the pungent floral smell. I rolled over on the damp earth, dewy grass sticking to my skin. I rubbed my eyes, trying to rid the deep slumber. I noticed my belongings were still next to me at the base of the hawthorn tree. But they were arranged in a haphazard way, as if they had been sorted through but whoever it was could not find what they were looking for. The branches adorned with white lace-like flowers drooped from the hawthorn – a sign winter is over and spring is here. An iridescent green bottle fly foraged upon the flowers, drawn to its scent that some say smells of death. Grabbing my kettle in one hand I began to pick leaves for my infusion, thanking the fairies with each plucking, for I know never to damage a hawthorn tree. The leaves are known to heal a broken heart and it is that broken heart that led me along a narrow woodland path just last night. The path adorned with bluebells and wild garlic eventually opened up into a vast meadow, with just one lone twisted hawthorn tree – the tree I fell asleep under. As I stooped down to grasp my stove I noticed a sparkle in the grass. Was it morning dew catching the sunlight? Then another, and another, followed by more dancing stars all around me. I heard a low hum from behind and turned. Landing on a white clover was a queen bumblebee and clutching the fur upon her back was a shimmering fairy queen. Gossamer wings, long auburn hair and a bluebell for a hat. Was it my broken heart or the hawthorn tree the reason she was here?

References

An Encyclopaedia of Plants in Myth, Legend, Magic and Lore by Stuart Phillips.

https://www.woodlandtrust.org.uk/trees-woods-and-wildlife/british-trees/a-z-of-british-trees/hawthorn/

Elinor and the Hawthorn by Julian Crooks

Recently her sleep had been increasingly disturbed, so much so that her dreams began to trouble her waking hours. But this walk had done her good. The further she walked through the fields, by the brook the more her mind seemed to clear itself. With each step her cares seemed to fall away. She stopped once more to listen. Yes, she was going in the right direction – the cuckoo, up ahead, called out again. It was clearly heading further up to the head of this curious valley. Behind her a crack of thunder echoed and, although she knew she would be drenched when she arrived back home (her mother casting a weather eye doubtfully skywards had predicted just this), Elinor carried on regardless.

Now a clearer path appeared by the side of the brook appearing to split neatly in two the great clouds of white cow parsley. The pungent, heady aroma of ransoms wafted from across the brook making her giddy. Elinor pressed on eagerly, ignoring her hunger, her light-headedness, taking little account of nettles and thistles now threatening to brush her bare arms.

The shock froze her mid-stride. Before her a stately hawthorn, crowned in white-frilled blossom. It stood imperious and impassive. She knew immediately that she had been enchanted. The cuckoo gazed down at her. It recognised her fatigue. 'You are weary,' it said. 'Rest your head awhile.' A sudden lethargy overcame her.

Elinor felt her legs buckling and found herself falling gently into a bed of soft, sweet-scented clover.

Many, many years afterwards she would explain to her grandchildren as best she could what had happened next. The details, she confessed, were left behind in that soporific nether world to which she had been magically invited. How the shimmering white lady, of modest and benign expression bid her enter the faerie kingdom; how she was attended by a host of tiny, gossamer-winged fays; how she was revived with a meal of the hawthorn's delicious, nutty leaves; how, much later, refreshed and invigorated and with a strength of purpose she had never experienced she had bid farewell to the lady, the hawthorn and the cuckoo. How she remembered the astonished face of her mother on her return; her mother's stare of disbelief at Elinor's clothes (somehow dry in spite of the thunderstorm) and of wonder at Elinor's long blonde tresses, newly bound and marvellously decorated with the beautiful blossom of the hawthorn.

All You Desire by Katherine Miskin

Once when it was still of use to wish for a thing, there was a night. And in the night was a sharp scent of tin, and a breath of icy air. The woods, so beautiful and safe in the day, were now infused with terror, and she hated herself for sleeping so long.

The ground now bony and hard, the air thick with strange noise. Shuffles and scuffles, breathy noises of unseen creatures. And she knew not to say the name of those who lived under this tree. They say the Gentry live under it. The Lords and Ladies. The Fair Folk. Whatever you do, you mustn't call on them, mustn't invite them in.

She longed to press her back into the tree, but the branches poked in many more directions than she remembered, and the thorns clasped at her hands as she felt around, tangled in her hair, and caught her clothes.

"What do you want?"

A voice of glass – a musical, tinkling, bright voice, but cold and hard. It's a voice whispering straight into her mind.

"What do you want, most in the whole world?"

Don't answer. Don't speak to it.

"What do you want, girl?"

The enchantment was too strong. She knew she mustn't, but she couldn't stop herself.

"I want to go home" she whispered in return.

The voice laughed. "Oh, but I can give you so much more than that! What do you want more than anything in the world? Beauty, love, gold? What do you want?"

Don't talk to them. Don't invite them in. Don't open your mind to them.

It laughed again. "I can see it already, why not tell me? I can see you wish for gold. You want to mend your father's house. You want to stop him struggling in the fields each day. I can give you all the gold you can carry."

She curled herself into a ball and tried to block the voice out with her fingers, but it cut straight into her head, laughing and mocking her.

"You only have to ask me, and I will give you gold."

When the sun rose, the girl was not there, just the dew drops hanging from the leaves of the hawthorn tree, each one heavy with the reflection of the golden sunlight.

The Lonely Black Bird by Nicky Hutchison

A long time ago, before memory began, there was a small dull bird who wore a dusty black coat. He had no friends and nobody to talk to and he lived his life pecking at seeds on the margins of a field. The bird looked as stern as anything but he was just sad and alone.

One day, he saw a commotion by a hedge disturbing his morning daydream. Two large, angry crows were mobbing a hare who was unable to escape their cruel beaks and razor talons. If he had had a chance to think about it this story would not exist but without thinking he flew at the two crows, stabbing at their eyes and flying so fast that it made them dizzy. The crows were so surprised at this ambush that they decided to leave the hare and fly off for something a bit more dead, like they normally did.

The hare was winded but unhurt and thanked her hero for his gallantry. In return, she said she would give her little champion his heart's desire. The bird was too shy to say what he really wanted, but the hare knew. First, she gave him the gift of tongues, the little bird opened his mouth and out came a chirruping clicking sound. He was so amazed he hopped about excitedly and puffed out his chest and twittered on for several minutes. The hare said that he would be a great mimic and would be able to converse with all beasts. She told him this would be useful for the long journey he needed to undertake.

The drab little birdie did not like the sound of a journey, indeed he once had a panic attack going beyond the confines of the field, but the wise-eyed hare said that to get what he truly wanted he had to be brave. She told him that as the sun set that very evening, he was to rise to the sky and fly once around the moon. Only then would he have everything he wished for. The bird ruffled his feathers in fear and looked dubiously up to the empty limitless heavens, his little heart beating wildly in his chest at the very thought. When he looked back the hare was gone.

Beset by self-doubt, but certainly no chicken, the wee bird searched his soul for guidance and by early evening he decided he had nothing to lose. Hoping nobody was looking, he launched himself into the high gloom, soared broad and wide and eventually rode the wind into the night sky and across to the silver moon. It was exhilarating to feel the icy breeze quiver his quills and he felt alive. As he glided nearer, the light from the moon blessed his feathers and his matt plumage became silky and lustrous. As he circled the moon, he touched the stars and millions of spots of light speckled his coat as he went by. On his way back he passed the sun and his beak absorbed its golden bounty. He sailed through the aurora and took on its myriad purples and greens as he rolled and whirled in rhythm with its hypnotic dance.

It was dusk again when the little bird arrived home. He chirped joyfully at his own prowess and audacity. He made such a noise and to-do that news soon spread of the bird with the marvellous mantle. All the little dull birds massed in the field to witness this wonder. Soon, the little black bird was flying with his like around the field. They swooped and swirled like the aurora itself to celebrate his magnificence and murmured that he was indeed the very best of birds. The now sheeny bird's tail feathers shook with pleasure and as they did so, millions of stars from his coat were cast abroad and landed on the rest of the flock until they glistened with stardust, moonlight and dawn clouds. They were all transformed!

The little bird was beautiful now and knew he would never feel lonely again. To this day, his sparkling flock gather every evening to soar and shimmer as one in the darkening sky. They would come to be known as starlings and became famous across the earth.

Hagstone Haggle by Katie Lloyd

The arc of the bay was encircled by indecisive weather – the centre of the beach was gifted the full spectrum of early spring colour by the sun, whilst the surrounding sea and land was overcome by great pillars of gilt-edged clouds.

The sea hissed and hushed as it pushed and pulled on the shingle shoreline. Oystercatchers piped to one another on rocky skerries and distant gannets plunged, like white arrows fired from angry gods, into the slate-coloured sea. A lone figure stood at the shoreline skimming pebbles.

The diminutive river babbled through folds of farmland and cut through a valley of limestone before spilling over pebble and stone to meet the ocean. A trail of willow, bramble, and old mossy stone walls edged the river on each side. A whitethroat was flushed from its willow-top singing perch and an unseen blackbird rattled an alarm call. A ripple of bracken tops betrayed the moving presence of something beneath. It stopped at an old stooped willow tree, which quivered and shook. A hand thrust a shiny black briefcase out of the foliage, followed by a trousered leg and the rest of a man, who emerged – with some difficulty – like a chick breaking the shell of its egg.

The man brushed down his suit, straightened his tie and strode towards the beach. Shiny leather shoes sunk into the shingle with every step. He stopped briefly to check his watch and mop sweat from his brow with a polka dot handkerchief. The air was still and humid, even here out on the beach.

He used his hands to balance as he clambered over the shingle bank and crunched with attempted composure over to the shoreline figure.

'This isn't an easy place to get to.' He said, as he approached, smoothing back his hair.

The young girl shrugged. 'It's how we like it.'

'So.' The man let the word linger in the still air.

'What is it you're after?' She asked eventually, eyes fixed on the sea as she skimmed another pebble.

'Well, hag stones, of course.'

She lowered the stone she was holding and turned to look at the man. Pigtails framed her stern look. 'Fertility? Healing? Safety for sailors? Protection of livestock...?'

'All of them.'

'They don't all do the same thing, you know. You're talking about a lot of hag stones there. And a lot of effort finding them.'

'That's why we've come to the very best.' He smiled at the girl, showing a set of straight, too-white teeth. 'And we're willing to pay the very best for it,' he tapped the briefcase.

She stared at him and then smiled, dimples filling her freckled cheeks. 'Tell you what,' she bent down and took something from inside her white ankle socks, 'take a look at this and see if we have a deal.' At that moment the pillows of clouds slid wide enough for a burst of sunlight to light up the whole bay and to illuminate the pure white stone on her palm.

He held it, captivated by the perfectly smooth round hole in its middle.

'That one is an all-rounder,' she said. 'But its speciality is warding off evil spirits.'

The man tilted his head back and held the stone up to the sky, as if he was checking the authenticity of a bank note. Sunlight squeezed through the hole and shone into the man's eyes. He turned away wincing, then looked again.

A gust of wind lifted off the waves, pulled at the man's tie and attempted to disturb his well-gelled hair. The girl took a lollipop out of her pocket and watched the man's eyes widen as he continued to gaze through the hole of the white hag stone. Overhead the clouds had gathered from all sides like a drawstring. The girl produced an umbrella and stood under its shelter sucking her lollipop as the first dollops of rain fell. The man shook his head, let out a gasping 'No!' and threw the white stone to the ground. 'Witch!' he shouted at the girl and turned so fast he fell into the shingle on all fours. 'Witch' he could still be heard shouting as he ran, stumbling back towards the river and diving through the willow scrub.

The girl pocketed the white hag stone and headed along the bay beneath parting clouds.

The briefcase, abandoned on the shingle, was pawed at by the incoming tide until, finally, it was sucked into its clutches.

The Legend of Wyre Forest and River Severn by Katie Lloyd

King Pumlumon lived on the highest hilltop in the west of Wales. He watched his Kingdom grow with each land claimed and with each turret added to his castle. He grew old and grey and made up for his withering looks with more and more emeralds which, on golden wires, hung from his robe and topped his towering crown.

One day the King was roaming through his domain, lamenting his bad luck in having seven daughters but never a son to hand down his wealth and power. On hearing the King, a nearby Serpent approached him with a deal – he could help him and the queen create a son if the King gave the Serpent enough emeralds to adorn his long body with. The King jumped at this offer and soon his wife became pregnant for an eighth time.

Nine months on, as the queen went into labour, the Serpent came to claim his jewels. 'There has been no boy's cry yet,' the King protested.

'It will be a boy, for I keep my promises,' the Serpent assured him. 'Now, an emerald for every inch of my long body.' The Serpent waited. The King smiled and gave the Serpent only enough emeralds to cover half of his body. Before the Serpent could complain, the King brought down his axe and cut the snake in two.

The Kingdom fell silent – for the queen and babe had died in labour. And the Serpent, hissing his revenge, found and ate all of the King's seven daughters. The Serpent fled the Kingdom, carving his way through the hills and lowlands and down to the English sea. The King, bereft, followed his path, crying with grief for his family. His tears filled the Serpent's trail, creating the mighty River of Severn.

The King, in his pursuit of the Serpent, reached a beautiful town which the Serpent had sliced in two. The townsfolk were so kind to the weeping King that, tired and weak, he decided to abandon his kingdom and his quest for vengeance, and spend his remaining days in this town he called Beaulieu – the beautiful place. Here, on his deathbed, the King cast aside his crown of golden wires and emeralds, creating Wyre Hill, upon which he spread his emerald-encrusted robe. In years to come this bore great majestic oaks and the emerald canopy of the Forest of Wyre. And within the Forest of Wyre serpents grew plentiful and large. And with every serpent that lives in the forest today, one can hear the ancient screams of seven sisters and the weeping of an old and greedy King.

The Uffington White Horse, Oxfordshire by Patricia Martin

Before the gods that made the gods
Had seen their sunrise pass,
The White Horse of the White Horse Vale
Was cut out of the grass
GK Chesterton, The Ballad of the White Horse 1911

There are many white horse figures carved on the chalk hillsides of southern England, particularly in Wiltshire. Along the ancient Ridgeway track, over the border in Oxfordshire, lies the oldest of all. Legend suggests that she is a mare and with her invisible foal beside her, she comes down at night to graze in the dip below the hill called The Manger, and to drink from the Woolstone Well, formed eons ago by her own hoofprint. Once every one hundred years, it is said, she gallops through the sky to Wayland who shoes her in his Smithy, an ancient landmark on the Ridgeway. The last time this occurred was reputedly in 1920, although there are no recorded eye-witnesses.

A century later, in 2020, on a dark night between moons, when the world was quiet, Wayland departed from his long held custom and left his Smithy to visit the mare, who stood quietly on the hillside while the blacksmith attended to her feet. Meanwhile, the foal, with the curiosity of all young animals, wandered softly away, quietly passing westwards along the grassy edge of the ancient trackway, his attention drifting towards he knew not what, his soft ears flicked forward, his little nostrils twitching as strange scents emerged from the darkness.

After a short distance, he left the track and moved upwards, stepping hesitatingly on his long cat-like legs over the deep springy turf until he reached the top of the hill called Hackpen, where the chalk land reaches its edge and drops steeply down an escarpment. Then the foal drew in his breath with a whispered gasp as he saw, on the hillside just below his feet the white shape of another horse, large and solid, carved on the steep chalk slope, a horse who forever looked over the flat claylands below. In the darkness the white horse raised his neck higher, turning his great white head towards the foal, his white ears pricked. The little horse watched him for a long tense moment, still, ready to flee. Then with a swirling of air, there was a galloping in the sky and in the darkness the mare arrived, her feet skimming the old turf and tracks, to encircle her foal, enveloping him with her care. She stood, turning her long, elegant neck to the white horse, and looked.

Then the ancient mare took her foal and faded into the darkness, moving back through the sky to take her place on her hillside with her foal invisible beside her before dawn spread over the land. But perhaps the movement of the air was gentler now as she travelled just a little more slowly away from end of the chalklands.

Under the Hawthorn Tree by Phoebe Devenney

I have no idea for how long I had been curled up under that Hawthorn Tree. It felt like it had been barely seconds for which I had closed my eyes before the strangeness started.

It was unusually warm for a Spring morning and the sun was shining a light so golden, it must have felt too cruel not to adorn every living soul in a shared glistening glow. The woods were effortlessly calm, like a lazy Sunday morning. The bees and butterflies bumbled their way between the foxgloves and old oak trees, going nowhere in particular in their most particular way.

Snuggled up in the cradling arms of the Hawthorn's branches, I was melting into the warming imaginings of life as a furry little bee when a rather painful tingling started to tip-toe across my nose. Naturally, I ignored the sensation, putting it down to a brief exposure to the dappled sunlight creeping through sheltering leaves. Instead, I embraced the solacing breeze that like my mother's breath, warmed my forehead with a kiss to tuck me into bed. Yet, such tranquillity had no place in this world of mischief.

The feeling suddenly intensified as the tingling progressed from a tap dancer's toes to an ice-skater's icy blades in a fuzzy, burning pain. I reached for my infliction only to be greeted by sticky fingers. I had a thick, gloopy substance fashioning a plush plum tone coating my wee button nose. Either the pigeons around these parts were hosting very interesting dinner parties or....

If it wasn't for her heaving sigh, I wouldn't have noticed her. She was quite unlike the fairies I had befriended in the picture books of my childhood. Unlike their dainty, thimble-like grace, Mopheline – as she liked to be known – clumped along in a clutter of awkward huffs and puffs. She reminded me of a fledgling in flight; frantic, clumsy and barely convincing even themselves that they know what they are doing.

Her button face was stained with the consequences of previous escapades. Flakes of mud, inky blackberry juice and splatters of sweat made her a suitable rival for Jackson Pollock's latest masterpiece. Her freckles, barely visible under the smudges and smears of her adventures, dotted her rounded little cheeks, mapping her bright eyes like twinkling stars. Oh to be an astrologer to those mischievous little eyes – what secrets you would unlock! That golden glint, almost lost beneath the mass of hair, that tangle of curls and twigs and frizz which bounced in the opposite direction to the rest of the world.

Her chaos was quite charming in an unexpected sort of way. Almost her punkish abandon and liberating sense of freedom was hard not to make you feel even just a little bit cheeky.

She hovered above a broken bit of bark whose jagged rim she had fashioned into a make-shift worktop that would make Mary Berry blush. The bubbled bark was hidden beneath fine powders, blobs and splatters, much like that which coated my nose. The ingredients seemed unrecognizable in their hairy-fairy heap sprawled across the desk. I couldn't help but wonder if she knew herself what she hurled into her cooking pot. She was hunched over a hollowed out conker which bubbled and spluttered away in a vigorous jig. Its shining husk bounced along the table as she threw substance after sticky substance into her glorious concoction.

Seeming satisfied with her choices, she used the prickle of a hedgehog to stir the bubbles and froth protruding from her pot, although, from the strain knitted into her furrowed brow and gritted teeth, it was a wonder if it was not the pot stirring her. She busied herself about her work with the same reckless carelessness of a child's play kitchen.

Suddenly, her darting ceased to only the ferocious flutter of her wings as with a tantalizing gulp, she halted her great efforts to sample her remedy. One surreptitious sip, a twitch of the eye as her cheeks began to swell as though fit to burst, I could hardly breath as I awaited the verdict. The sound of a guzzle as clear as an acorn dropping on wood erupted into a whirlwind of wails, snorts and sniffles as she collapsed into a snivelling mound. The acorn cap she wore for a hat teetered with each shaking breath and abruptly, the world felt a little colder, a little darker and a lot less fun.

I gently asked her what was the matter as I handed her a Hawthorn petal for her to blow her nose on.

"It's awl g-gwarn wrong..." she sniffled as she took a heffalump's blow on her hanky. Then out it all spluttered with slurring syllables, reddened cheeks and flaring nostrils. "It is the spwing t-time ball t-tonight and I'm m-making the punch to celbwate the n-new season. My Gwanny usually m-makes it and I've lost her wrecipe. I c-can't work out what-s m-missing!"

I felt a deep, hollowing emptiness as I heard her hiccoughing breath and saw her trembling hands. There must be something I could do?

Like the most joyful epiphany, my mother's voice rang through my head as I remembered our walks through sun-kissed meadows so long ago. I thought of the wisdom she shared and the stories of the flowers she told to me with so much love. I thought of the daisies and their symbol of life, of motherhood; purity and new beginnings. As if holding her hand, with courage I said: "Why not try adding the magic of a daisy."

As if a candle had been lit in that little heart of hers, she began to radiate a glow of more treasure than words can do justice. With endless thanks and jubilation, back to her work Mopheline fluttered. Such magic, such joy that only the woodland could harvest.

From that moment on, I knew that it would be a day I would want to live in forever, but to say what happened next, now, that would be telling...

Searching for Finn by Charlotte Dale

The giant woke from his slumber rubbing the rocks of sleep from his eyes. As he inhaled a yawn the sand and shale whipped up in a vortex around him. His exhalation caused tidal waves across the Atlantic Ocean and tremors could be felt all the way down Antrim Bay. He rolled over and every creature along the shores of the Inner Hebrides read the vibrations. They knew what was coming and clung to rocks and each other like limpets.

Finn still made the journey here regularly but the result was always the same – Benandonner could never be found. *How can a giant so big hide?* Unsteady on his feet Finn stood like a toddler wobbling on the rocks. He inhaled and looked across the Atlantic, "home" he murmured as rock pools quivered. Standing taller than the cliffs, one foot in front of the other, his shoes as big as cars. Slowly he thumped along the beach to the shoreline crushing shells in his wake. "Home" – this time louder, lower. A frequency only the whales could hear. He entered the water, having to paddle as the Causeway had been ripped up. A mile out to sea as the cold Atlantic reached his thighs, his arms swayed back and forth, stirring the ocean – and the waves could be felt from Rosslare to The Clyde.

Benandonner's Revenge by Julian Crooks

Finn, the great giant of Ireland, had defeated Benandonner. But it was not a victory of which he was proud. Benandonner had retreated back across the causeway to Scotland scooping up great swathes of the basalt columns as he went, flinging them miles away into the sea, intent on ensuring he could not be pursued by the mighty Finn. He did not know he had been duped. He was unaware that Finn was not as mighty as he. By pretending to be the baby of Finn the Irish giant had fooled his Scottish rival into assuming that Finn was monstrously, inconceivably huge! In reality it was Finn who was much the smaller of the two.

Although Finn's wife had saved her husband's life by dressing him as a baby, she was weary of his childlike behaviour and dependence on her. 'You're supposed to be a giant,' she would tell him, 'it's about time you acted like one!' It was almost as though Finn wanted to be a baby! Finn, had even taken to hiding in a cave at the base of the cliffs adjoining the Causeway. He was convinced that Benandonner would discover the truth and seek revenge. Although it was a tight squeeze, the cave, which ran deep under the towering cliffs, was the only place he felt safe.

Truth be told, Bel had become dissatisfied with her marriage to this 'would be' giant and, having set eyes on Benandonner, ruggedly handsome, athletic and muscular, adorned in his splendid furs and kilt she had liked what she had seen and she began to ponder.

Perhaps now was the time to ditch the Irish and see what a bit of Scotch could do for her.

The distance from the Causeway across the North Channel to Kintyre is a mere twenty miles which is nothing to the seabirds which regularly flit back and forth across the sea as they scour the heaving waters for shoals of herring and mackerel. So it was that one day Bel had words with a sly Bonxie* newly arrived from Scotland. Sure enough the message was passed on to Benandonner the very next day. Benandonner's fury was unbounded. How dare Finn make such a fool of him – pretending to be a mere baby to trick him!

Bel, meanwhile, had suggested to Finn that he best make the cave his permanent home – if he was so certain that Benandonner would return it was the only place a giant could hide on this bare stretch of coastline. She prepared a meal of Finn's favourite dish – puffin and guillemot pie served with her own special peppered porpoise sauce. Finn smacked his huge lips together when he caught the delicious aroma and, saliva oozing from the corners of his mouth, he willingly crept into the darkest recesses of the cave, taking great care not to spill the tiniest morsel from the dish he carried.

Once settled at the back of the cave, black as night and as silent as the moon, Finn began to enjoy his meal. His tastebuds became exceptionally sensitive as his sight (in the pitch black) and hearing (in the silence) were not needed. Strange it was though, that he could not detect the grating and sliding of boulders and columns at the cave's entrance. Bel had let Benandonner know that Finn would be captive in the cave and she had set about blocking the entrance. All Benandonner had to do was to remove the boulders and columns, reach in with his long arms and drag out the poor, defenceless Finn by one of his puny legs. She could picture her Scottish hero dangling aloft her erstwhile husband like a bunch of grapes before he flung him with a mighty sweep of his wonderfully biceped arm to the far side of the world! Then, she reflected, Benandonner would be hers and the union of Ireland and Scotland could begin!

As we all know these proud nations were never united as one and this is why. Whilst Finn was only halfway through his meal Benandonner arose majestically from the sea, stepping up the remains of the column causeway, dripping water. Bel, atop the cliff nearly fainted at the sight. So regal, so magnificent! Like Neptune himself arising from the deep. Soon he would be hers!

Bending down at the base of the cliff Benandonner discovered the blocked cave entrance and was about to extract, like a handful of matchsticks crammed into a mousehole, the columns when a rumble could be heard from deep within the cliff. Benandonner paused, his brow furrowed. The rumbling grew louder, became a roar and then... the cliff seemed to explode from within. Bel, was shot far up into the air and through the clouds, an enormous gaping hole in the cliff where she had been sitting. Finn, inhaling just a teeny bit too much of the delicious pepper sauce had blown the top out of the cliff with a truly gigantic sneeze.

    Startled beyond belief by this unexpected turn of events Benandonner retreated once more to his native Scotland, never to return. Finn survived the cave collapse and vowed never to let his wife talk him into anything again. Bel eventually landed in a fjord and was rescued by a short-sighted troll who claimed her for his own. And when you do visit the Giant's Causeway just be careful of the view from the cliffs above – the deep, dangerous blowhole remains to claim the unwary. Locals say on a still evening when the draught from the cave below seeps up you might still catch the sharp aroma of peppered porpoise.

*Bonxie – *the local's name for the great skua*

The Revenge of the Giant by Phoebe Devenney

Raging, rumbling, thundering and blundering.

Spit and spray of deep murky waters

Through the cracks came crashing,

Came foaming and fuming,

Spluttering and smouldering.

Fists and teeth and bloodshot eyes

With anger, with pain, with unforgiving threat,

Come to intrude the Giant's place of rest.

For years he had slumbered;

His snores had been stifled by the waves' bashing tones,

But now the air was filled with his thirst for bones.

Grumbles, groans, rumbles and moans.

Twitching, stretching, clenching, awakening.

He was stiff, he was sore and oh how he ached,

But none compared to the land forsaked.

He brushed off the villages that had made home on his fist,

He kicked away his snow-topped knees as he drew them out of the mist.

As for the fishermen's coves that sheltered between his toes:

Down they all clattered, torn out and battered.

The roads across his chest cracked with each passing breath

As guttural sighs and burnt-out cries sang across the seas.

As clicking and cracking, heaving and huffing,

As chewing and licking, grinding and biting,

He stands above his land, his fine, magnificent land

And thinks of the pain he shall cause with a simple brush of his hand.

SCIENCE FICTION WRITING

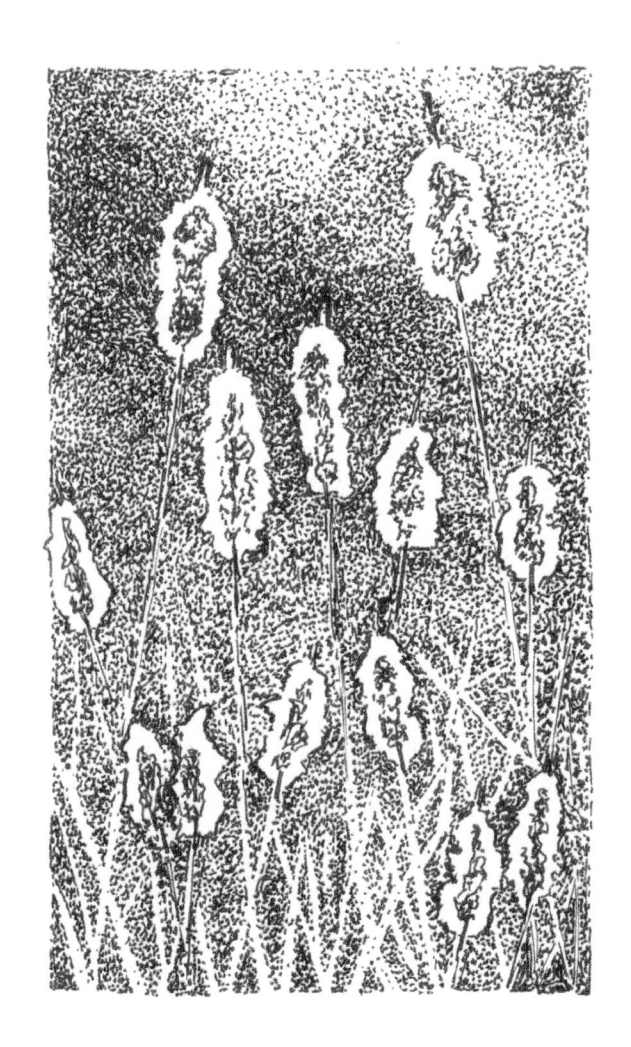

Introduction: Science Fiction Writing

Approaching genres such as science fiction can be a daunting prospect for new writers. Many people wouldn't immediately think that science fiction writing would work well linked together with nature writing, however the natural world is a rich resource of material that can inspire the most unusual forms of science fiction.

We only need to spend an afternoon searching up sea creatures from the deep to find hundreds of strange and unusual species, perfect for any fantasy or science fiction setting. The qualities we find in plants and animals can be combined with human or alien species to invent some incredible characters.

We can also use science fiction writing to consider what it means to be human. I am lucky enough to have worked alongside a brilliant project called *Terra Two*. Terra Two is a writing project being led by Liesl King at York St John University. The aim is to 'shape the first off world settlement through the lens of science fiction'[10]. Considering what humans need beyond basic survival is a great way to think about the importance of our current world. We worked on a task that asked writers to imagine that they were being moved to a different planet. They were allowed to choose one species of plant (not essential to survival) to take with them. The final three pieces of work in this anthology are a response to

---

[10] **www.Yorkstjohnterratwo.com**

this task. They are thought provoking and a great way to consider the incredible species in the world in which we live.

Kindred Spirit by Sharon Williamson

You wouldn't have thought it would be a difficult thing to choose. 'One plant per colonist,' the information said. But which should I take?

This was the most exciting, and the most daunting, of times. I had been selected for a new off-world colony, given the opportunity to start a whole new chapter in my life. It meant leaving behind a lot of things, both good and not so good. But it was the choice of a plant that was occupying me for the moment. Classic displacement activity, I thought to myself.

The colony would be self-sufficient in many things, food being one – edible plants would be grown in hydroponic modules, so I didn't need to worry about growing my own potatoes, or rice, or fruit. Hydroponics would be growing things like bamboo, too, for fibres and structural needs. I could take something more personal. But what?

I considered a rose, elegant and fragrant when in flower, a reminder of the gardens of old Earth. Perhaps some herbs – oregano or basil maybe – to add to whatever the standard fare would be; that felt like a possibility. In the end, sheer pragmatism won the day. I found a plant that was robust, a survivor, but with the potential for an unexpected show of beauty, one day. I almost felt it was a kindred spirit: a cactus.

No Place Like Home by Charlotte Dale

When I first stepped down onto the powdery grey surface, I expected clouds of dust – but nothing. It didn't even stain my space suit. It was like we were actors in an old black-and-white film. Black above, grey below and we all wore white space suits. In single file we followed the captain with our precious cargo – one plant or tree each.

Feeling a stone heavier and carrying my beloved tea rose I turned round to view the long line behind me. Everyone's head bowed; somehow it made walking easier, as if we were walking into an invisible wind. The eclectic mix of foliage ranged from tiny seedlings to tall young saplings, some in bloom and some in bud like my rose.

My tea rose had caused quite a heated discussion on the journey here – it wasn't just this planet's atmosphere that was cold and icy. "Why have you brought that? We're going to need food," was one remark. Followed by "how selfish" and "what use is that?" But I had no regrets. And as we entered the 'growing hub' (a huge poly tunnel with bright white lights), I knew I'd made the right choice. The horticultural team in green space suits had been busy preparing the beds – rotted down organic matter mixed with the planet's grey dust. Lots of vegetation had already been planted but there was much more to be done. But as I looked around at the people in their green suits holding long paint brushes, their buzzing pollinating sticks, I knew once this tea rose was in bloom, we would all be grateful for its sight and scent. Because here there were no bees or pollinators – and that just makes me want to go home.

How Not to Conquer a Planet by Julian Crooks

Captain's Log, Stardate 26-2-15.8

This is my last log before the ship lands on Alpha Centaur Delta Cosmos (ACDC). After waking up yesterday (or was it a week last Wednesday? These so called 'galactic days' are so much longer than your normal earth days) I've had time to check the sample pods to ensure all the seeds and items needed for the hedge-laying are ready and the built-in germination and flowering programmes are functioning. To be honest I had to read through the mission instructions a few times to remind myself precisely what I was supposed to be doing in this too far flung, furthest reach of the galaxy – 52,000 light years (or thereabouts) is quite a long time to travel in cryostasis and as this is a solo mission there's no one around to ask. Well, there is Jig-Jag of course, but I've fallen out with it already – I mean, who wants a know-it-all robot around watching your every move? And frankly I don't care if he has the complete wealth of human knowledge accessible on its hard drive, sometimes things are just better left to good old human instinct.

So the plan for tomorrow: after touch down we take advantage of the darkness (a fifty-five hour night) to release the samples. Jig-Jag will travel 30 kilometres and then begin sowing the seeds in a ten metre wide trench which will encircle the landing base. The idea is to grow a protective hedge to keep out the native aliens while we (that is I) get on with our business of establishing the newest trading post this side of the Gamma galaxy.

Captain's Log Stardate 26-2-15.9

From planet ACDC. All going according to plan. Jig-Jag has successfully sown the seeds. The effort has drained its battery however and it's now recharging. The plants are doing marvellously. Most are now at full height, budding and about to flower. They were carefully selected of course: holly, floribunda rose and belladonna – the perfect botanical mixture of beauty and pain! Lovely to behold but injurious by nature. Those disgusting snotty-green alien residents (when they finally do awake and come for a look at their new invader) are in for quite a shock. Naturally, they will have to breach the hedge. When they try to grasp the attractive glossy leaves of the holly they'll be prickled and stabbed; as they reach for the lusciously perfumed salmon-pink bloom of the rose they will find their skin ripped to shreds by the thorns and as they attempt to peer closely at the delicate petals of the nightshade they will receive a wonderfully toxic dose of the latest nerve agent. Both of the planet's suns have now risen and we have daylight of sorts as it's actually quite misty and difficult to see too much. I wonder how long the aliens will be before they decide to turn up and attempt to meet and parley with their conqueror?

Captain's Log Supplemental

Jig-Jag having regained sufficient battery power now tells me that the resident aliens have the capability to shape-shift. Apparently, they can transform themselves from the regulation 'little green men' as illustrated in our manuals into particles of gas and float around wherever they wish. This seems a little unfair to me and definitely not cricket. Furthermore, Jig-Jag asserts that the aliens have at their disposal an amazing array of extra-terrestrial trickery which includes altering the properties and appearance of any carbon-based life forms. I could swear that Jig-Jag sniggered as it told me this alarming fact.

Captain's Log Stardate 26-2-16

Jig-Jag was right. These aliens are much cleverer than I dare imagined. They have used their cosmic wizardry to de-prickle the holly leaves, turn the rose thorns into little nodules and de-poison the belladonna. So much for mankind's grand plans. For a robot Jig-Jag has remarkably human sensibilities; he is adamant that he is done with conquest and would like to settle here on ACDC. I'm off to consult the Galactic Atlas – there must be easier worlds to conquer.

About the Editors:

Emma McKenzie

Emma is a freelance writer and artist who lives in York. Emma designed and led the two creative writing courses for the Field Studies Council, which inspired this anthology. You can find out more about Emma's current adventures at:

www.lifeatbasecamp.com

Twitter: @slicesofmylife

Instagram: @em_creative

Julian Crooks

Julian is an English teacher and lives in South Yorkshire. He is a keen birdwatcher and enjoys exploring landscapes and discovering nature at every opportunity. Julian attended both Emma's courses with the FSC and worked with Emma to produce this anthology.

About the Writers:

Rebecca Banks

Rebecca lives with her family in rural Staffordshire, where she regularly connects with nature through writing, dog walking and foraging. She has worked in the environmental sector for 20 years and now runs her own ethical business supporting people to connect with nature in a way that feels right for them. To find out more
visit https://www.facebook.com/CommunityForestServicesLtd

Sarah Carlin

Sarah Carlin started nature writing during lockdown as a way to reconnect with the world outside her window. Living in a big city she enjoys watching the way nature finds a way to survive and thrive, in spite of the urban sprawl.
Follow on: sarah.carlin.home@instagram.com

Jenny Cooper

Jenny Cooper has grown up with nature, living in rural Suffolk. She is happiest walking her dogs or being in the woods, listening and watching the flora and fauna. She has enjoyed learning more about creative writing through taking part in the Field Studies Council courses.

Charlotte Dale

Charlotte Dale has always been in awe of the natural world – especially bees. She's volunteered for the RSPB and BBCT but after becoming ill in 2018 her garden is now her sanctuary. She enjoys writing and many natural history courses with the Field Studies Council. (You can find out more about Charlotte and nature through the seasons at thebackgardennaturalist.wordpress.com)

Phoebe Devenney

Phoebe Devenney is a young artist inspired by nature and all things wild and a little bit magical. She has always enjoyed writing and loved taking part in the FSC writing course to explore her passion for the natural world in a different creative way. Learning and collaborating with other writers helped her to develop a joy of the written word, whilst broadening an appreciation of new skills and inspiration from the world and the beautiful life within it. Phoebe will continue to reflect on the ideas provoked by the course through her art and writing.

Elizabeth Fairweather

Elizabeth Fairweather has enjoyed exploring new ideas about creative writing through taking part in the FSC course. Elizabeth currently lives in King's Lynn, Norfolk, and after a period of illness, is trying to get back into a regular habit of connecting to nature through words and photographs. She has a nature blog: elizabethswildlifeblog.wordpress.com

Nicky Hutchison

Unsuited to the stresses and strains of city life into which she was born, and too mean for expensive clinics and therapies, Nicky Hutchison rehabilitated herself using a home-grown nature cure of running and walking in the countryside. She was finally released into the wild in the Forest of Dean where she continues to ramble on in poetry and prose.

Sharon Linden

Sharon Linden is new to nature writing. The Field Studies Council's 'Introduction to Nature Writing' course has been a real inspiration to her, and she continues to write based on observing, and connecting with the natural world about her.

Katie Lloyd

Katie Lloyd is a conservation biologist whose work inspires her writing and illustrations. She enjoys combining her passions for words, art and nature and likes to use her writing to inform and enthuse others. She has contributed to BBC Wildlife magazine and several ecology publications, and owns a secret stash of unfinished poems.

Patricia Martin

Patricia Martin lives in rural North Wiltshire and has long wanted to write effectively about the wildlife and countryside around her. Being new to nature writing, she really appreciated the support and positive encouragement provided by Emma and the other students on the Field Studies Council course.

Katherine Miskin

Katherine took up writing whilst on part time furlough at the start of 2021. She is based in North Bedfordshire where she works for an environmental conservation charity and is inspired by the land around her and people's interaction with it.

Steven Mitchell

Steven Mitchell is a writer of short stories and novels based in St Albans, Herts. Always happier outdoors than in, he took the Field Studies Council Nature Writing course to develop his nature writing skills to use in his fiction. His debut novel, *Under The Moss*, is published by SRL. Steven is the chair of the 67-year-old Verulam Writers group. www.stevenmitchellwriter.com

Hilary Park

Hilary Park is a designer and writer. Her work is inspired by the landscape and wildlife of Westmorland where her studio is based. The FSC nature writing course was a welcome opportunity to read, write and learn in the company of like-minded writers. Hilary is currently developing her fiction writing and illustrating a poetry pamphlet.

Kate Stacey

Kate Stacey lives in Cumbria and started writing about nature whilst commuting, when she attempted to describe the scenery she saw through the train window. She enjoyed learning more on the Field Studies Council's nature writing class and is continuing to explore words to capture the nature she loves and the landscape that surrounds her.

Suzanne Thomas

Suzanne Thomas is a storyteller and folklorist living in South Shropshire. She tried her hand at Nature Writing after reading several books of that genre during the first of the Covid lockdowns. In Autumn 2021 she began a blog where she tries to capture the changing mood of the landscape and seasons at silvestrispath.wordpress.com

Berenice Tregenna

Berenice Tregenna (@berietree) writes the 'Berie Tree' nature blog: http://www.berrietree.wordpress.com This blends art and science to raise awareness for common insects and plants. She sees herself as 'Nature's Magnifier', highlighting the hidden wealth of our natural surroundings. She also takes nature photos and posts them on social media. She aims to encourage people to appreciate nature and help the environment.

Sharon Williamson

Sharon Williamson is a freelance editor living in rural Cambridgeshire. She keeps a nature journal, and leads nature journalling sessions locally. She loves drawing and sketching inspired by the natural world, and thoroughly enjoyed the challenge of the FSC nature writing courses.

Sharon's blog, Cambridgeshire Nature Notes, is at http://cambsnaturenotes.blogspot.com/, and her artwork can be seen at https://www.instagram.com/sharoncambs/

Getting Started on Nature Writing

Starting a Nature Journal:

A great way to begin writing about the natural world is to start a nature journal. It can be any book shape, or size. Some writers choose pages that are not lined to allow for sketching and painting alongside words. Other writers like to use their journals to press flowers and leaves amongst the pages.

Consider your writing routine, how often will you write, where will you write? Choose a journal that suits your practice. For someone who likes to journal on the move, recording little observations and details along the way, something that fits in your pocket would work better than a large book. If you are going to create a nature journal from home you might prefer something larger that you can dedicate more creative time to.

Here are some tasks you might like to consider for your journal:

1. <u>Sketching with words:</u>
Choose any natural object and try to describe it in detail, without naming it. Use your senses (sight, sound, smell, touch) to explore the object in detail. You might want to use metaphors to liken your object to something else to create a

visual picture. Play with different styles of writing to see how accurately you can describe your item.

2. <u>Exploring species:</u>
Choose something that stands out to you in nature, such as birds, trees, flowers etc. Use your journal to record different types of a given species. What do you notice about each one? Where did you see it? What type of environment does it like? You can also use your journal to include research notes on your given species and to press examples of petals or leaves etc.

3. <u>Daily journaling:</u>
Set aside time to nature journal on a regular basis (I would suggest 5–10 minutes a day to get started). This might be at the end of a morning walk, or choosing a quiet time to observe a scene from your window every day. This can be as simple as charting the birds on the rooftops (if you are in a built up area), to recording a beautiful landscape and how it shifts through the seasons. You will be surprised what you notice and the differences that you see once you start to record things and build a relationship with the natural world.

If you are interested in joining the Field Studies Council courses please visit: https://www.field-studies-council.org . Alongside the creative writing courses there are arts and photography courses, as well as many different courses exploring different habitats and species that will increase your knowledge and inspire new writing.

Useful Links and Resources

Field Studies Council: https://www.field-studies-council.org

The Haiku Foundation: https://thehaikufoundation.org

Poetry Foundation: https://www.poetryfoundation.org

Woodland Trust: https://www.woodlandtrust.org.uk has a wealth of information on different types of trees, alongside beautiful videos capturing different trees changing through the seasons.

Royal Society for the Protection of Birds: https://www.rspb.org.uk is a great place to find out more about our feathered friends. You can also find out details of RSPB nature reserves and where to see different species.

Terra Two project at York St John University: https://yorkstjohnterratwo.com/about/

The Wildlife Trusts: https://www.wildlifetrusts.org If you are interested in supporting your local environment and learning more about species across the UK, the Wildlife Trusts has 2,300 different sites to explore, a fantastic way to find local areas to support your writing development.

Printed in Great Britain
by Amazon